Love at Second Sight
Playing the Midlife Dating Game

Love at Second Sight
Playing the Midlife Dating Game

Nancy W. Collins
and Mason Grigsby

New Horizon Press
Far Hills, New Jersey

New Horizon Press
P.O. Box 669
Far Hills, NJ 07931

Nancy W. Collins and Mason Grigsby
    Love at Second Sight: Playing the Midlife Dating Game

Cover Design: Mike Stromberg
Interior Design: Susan M. Sanderson

Library of Congress Control Number: 20030105870

ISBN: 0-88282-247-0 New Horizon Press

Manufactured in the U.S.A.

2007   2006   2005   2004   2003   /   5   4   3   2   1

TABLE OF CONTENTS

FOREWORD

Immature love says: "I love you because I need you."
Mature love says: "I need you because I love you."

Erich Fromm
The Art of Loving

Until recently, textbooks on developmental psychology ran out of gas after describing how adolescent humans made the big break from their families of origin and their familial roots. The implication was that after that break, the adult was fully formed and further change or development was minimal. The baby boomer generation, with all of its self-absorption and applied energy, has put an end to that assumption. Now, developmental psychology includes a field known as Adult Development, which attends to the continuing growth of people on, into and through a stage previously referred to as "middle age."

The one thing that we thought we knew about the midlife period was that men were inclined to start jogging and buy red Corvettes to demonstrate that they were not yet over the hill. Women didn't need to indulge in such foolishness, as they were happily engaged with their children, grandchildren and a little gardening. Hard to believe, but such hackneyed clichés were accepted as fact.

We now know that these stereotypes are untrue. There is a powerfully rich experience to be found in our middle years, one that is accompanied by considerable wisdom of experience. Mature adults have been around the block, sure, but unlike their not-too-distant ancestors, many have disposable income, good health and a restless kind of energy. They are unlike some of their predecessors in another important way: many are single. Today, fewer people remain in marriages that are imperfect or unfulfilling. Their parents may have stayed in such marriages, as it was more difficult and less acceptable to divorce in the past. But many boomers watched their parents suffer and decided that marital prisons were not for them, so they delayed marriage altogether or got themselves out of dysfunctional unions.

Social and developmental changes are rarely smooth or painless, though, and the freedoms of the last half of the twentieth century have not come without stresses and difficulties for many. This book addresses one of the problems associated with these dramatic changes: How do you find a good, romantic relationship when you are in your forties, fifties or older? Is it just as hard or just as easy for you as it was when you were in high school? Does it happen in the same way? Are the rules basically the same—or have they changed?

Nancy Collins and Mason Grigsby have done their homework on this subject in two essential ways. First, they report from the trenches of midlife dating and the male/female relationship wars. They've been there and they know the rules of engagement. They share their veteran's stories that are well worth a listen. Second, they have asked others to share their experiences, using a series of 400 in-depth surveys and follow-up interviews with over 1,000 single people, which provided a wealth of instructive examples. Some are cautionary tales; some are magical stories of relationship wonder.

Their central idea is thought provoking: When, at a young age, you first began interacting with people from that other gender, you had no idea what was going on. You were clueless, hoping against hope for luck in finding the perfect partner and forming a successful marriage. You were young and probably had no real idea who you were, what you liked and what your bad habits could turn out to be. More than likely, you had few accurate ideas about the other gender. Your head was full of fantasy nonsense gleaned from pop culture images. You were brainwashed by stories like *Cinderella* and movies like *Gone with the Wind*, *My Fair Lady* and *Casablanca* and songs by the Temptations (*My Girl*), Connie Francis *(Where the Boys Are)* and the Beach Boys *(California Girls)*. Your view of gender roles may have been shaped by your wrestling coach, the nuns at your school or good old mom and dad. You were in for a rough ride, indeed!

You persevered, however, and you gave it your best shot. You dated, you married, you raised your kids, you got them through high school or college. Maybe you paid for their weddings and perhaps even the down-payment on a house. If your marriage worked out well, if you and your spouse are closer and more deeply in love than you ever were, this book is not for you. Close it and feel lucky. Keep doing whatever it is that you do so well.

If, however, you are one of the many others who, sooner or later, threw in the towel on your marriage, or if you unfortunately suffered the death of a spouse or if you never got married at all, you may find this book to be useful, indeed. Nancy and Mason maintain that you are in a terrific position, because now in your maturity, you know much more about who you are and what you want. You don't need to operate in the dark, as you did in your twenties. You don't need to waste time looking for love in all the wrong places or ways.

The authors' second essential point is this: The boat is leaving the dock, maybe for the last time. As they say, "You can't wait around for tomorrow—it is tomorrow!" You may have the wisdom that comes with age, but you no longer have the luxury of time on your side. You must act. You must take risks if you hope to enhance your relationship life. You can't sit at home and mope, you can't go to the same old places wearing the same old clothes and you can't do the same thing you have been doing and expect magically different results. Changes need to be made, particularly in how you think of yourself and what you are looking for in a romantic partner.

This book is also useful because it outlines a dating strategy, something the authors refer to as a "Game Plan," based upon the basics of backgammon. There's a Beginning Game, a Middle Game and an End Game, which they describe in detail with real-life examples. They even provide specific scripts in some cases, the exact words you can use to get what you want. They offer advice about food, dress, dating customs, sexual etiquette and a primer on how to effectively use technology to your dating advantage. For example, they recommend that you "Google" someone on the Internet before you commit much time to him or her. This advice has two specific benefits. First, you might find out that your Prince or Princess is a loser, or worse, a dangerous person. Second, you might get a few wonderful conversation starters. ("You wrote a piece that was published in *Atlantic Monthly*, didn't you?")

This book does something else that it may not have started out to do: It explains aspects of the male and female personality that academic psychology seems to have missed. The honest writing provides unvarnished insights into what men think about women and what women desire in men, romance, dressing up and first dates. Both sexes desiring mates should pay attention.

For instance, if you are a recalcitrant male, there are spots in the book where straight advice is given. "Listen," the authors say, "you can't go out looking like a slob and expect women to take an interest in you." And stop bragging. Women don't want to hear it. They won't be impressed and they won't put up with it the way they did in their twenties. One piece of advice is especially priceless for middle-aged men: When you open your mouth to complain about how your body is breaking down, how stiff you feel, how you can't play sports like you used to…put a sock in it! Women don't want to hear a long-winded discourse on your bout with midlife trials and tribulations. This same advice, to eliminate talk of the way your body has shifted shape or how you can't play sports any more however, goes for women too.

Grigsby and Collins assert that in order to succeed in the midlife relationship world both men and women must take risks. In order to do this, however, you must have self-confidence. If by this point in your life you don't have adequate self-confidence, it might be a good idea to get some help. Assistance is available in many forms: in self-help books, in groups and in therapy. Now that you have matured, you probably have some extra money to spend on yourself and there is no reason to be afraid or too proud to seek help. Good therapy, done with an empathic and competent counselor, can be one of life's real treasures. Shop around until you find a therapist with whom you are comfortable. Then get to work. It's not too late to make important positive changes that can lead to twenty or more years of happiness. Few investments yield something that valuable.

Consider the price of this book and the time you spend reading it an investment in your future. Written explicitly for men and women in their mid-years who are interested in developing relationship and dating savvy, it is an insider's book written by two people who have walked the walk and talked the talk. Begin today to put their advice and suggestions to work for you and learn how to be a winner in the midlife dating game.

Bruce Peltier, Ph.D.

Bruce Peltier, PhD, MBA, is a clinical psychologist and author of *The Psychology of Executive Coaching*.

PART 1

The Beginning Game: How to Start

Introduction

Finding yourself single in midlife can be one of life's greatest challenges. This is especially true if you have been in a loving, nurturing and intimate relationship. If the relationship ends abruptly, due to death, divorce or if one of the partners simply opts to leave, there can be an intense and prolonged period of emotional upheaval before recovery can begin. If there is much grief, there often needs to be a physical as well as an emotional healing. Regardless of the elapsed time after the event, the overwhelming majority of the 400 participants in our study of mature singles told us they experienced a powerful urge to begin looking for a new partner.

Looking for a new partner and finding him or her are two different stories, however. Why is it so difficult in midlife to find the "right" person? We may have a picture of that perfect person tucked away in the corners of our minds, but later, when we find ourselves ready to make a commitment, the person rarely resembles, either physically or emotionally, the one we thought we were seeking.

According to the 2002 Census, there are over forty-two million people in the United States who are over forty and single. For those of us who fit into that demographic, midlife dating offers totally different challenges than did the youthful dating/marriage scenarios of our twenties. In those days neither men nor women had much knowledge of what a dating relationship meant for the future. But now, as mature adults, we want to understand where we are going in relationships and why. We want to be a bit more clear-headed than we were in our youth. And since many of us have been out of the dating game for some time, we need a new set of skills, guides and a strategy that will make us successful players.

Backgammon is probably the best example of a game with a beginning game strategy, a middle game strategy and an end game strategy. Similarly, in dating there is a Beginning Game, a Middle Game and an End Game. We have organized this book into these three segments with behavioral examples that illustrate each of these stages of the dating game.

While backgammon is sometimes a game of luck, it is mostly a game of skill and the most skillful player will almost always win. Skilled players have studied the game and have become experts as to what strategies produce successful results. Consequently, they are consistent winners, losing only to equal or better players. The player counting on luck alone will win only occasionally, if at all.

So it is with dating in midlife. If you have no knowledge of the newer concepts and requirements for communicating with the opposite sex, you will find yourself dating the wrong people or being rejected time and time again—for reasons you do not understand. If you fit this bill, there is a reason for your relationship mishaps and it may be your lack of a focused strategy and an ability to play the game according to the new rules of contemporary dating.

Knowing when to "stay" and when to "drop" is considered one of the most important elements of the game of Backgammon. Understanding what course of action is appropriate in the beginning, middle and end of the game, when to drop and cut your losses and when to stay and increase your risks is essential to any player's strategy. Similarly, in dating, there will be a point in time in which the person you have been seeing wants to make the relationship exclusive. You will have to make a decision to accept, and "stay," or to "drop" out of the relationship. This book will help you formulate a winning strategy.

In the Beginning Game, which we discuss in Part I of the book, the initial date signifies the start of the game. This means paying more attention to the all-important first impression, as the rules of engagement at this level are critical. More than ever, people of both sexes are relying on first meetings to form opinions. Most people in midlife do not want to waste time and have little tolerance for what they consider inappropriate behavior. This is the time to put all the knowledge and experience you have learned from past relationships into use.

For example, on a first date, one of the questions frequently asked by both men and women is, "Are you looking for a serious, monogamous relationship?" The operative word here is "looking." Ideally, neither party should be "looking" for a relationship; each individual should be living a life that has joy, purpose and meaning.

The correct response to the question should be something to the effect of, "I have a good life and am very happy with what I am doing. I am not 'looking' for a relationship or marriage, but I would certainly welcome one if the right person entered my life."

This reply indicates you do not need to be rescued by a relationship. It says you are okay, self-confident, self-assured and are open to a relationship, but you are not desperately seeking someone to act as a salvation from your current life. This is the basic message of the Beginning Game—you have a life, but are open to a new relationship; you are not looking and you are not needy. And this is the answer most well adjusted single people will welcome.

Remember, with almost forty-two million single men and women over the age of forty milling around out there, the odds of meeting someone compatible are very good. The vast majority of them aren't happy being alone either. In fact, the number one priority for the majority of the respondents in our survey is "to find a great relationship." So with all those single people out there, at least one of them is looking for you.

Playing the game of backgammon, knowing when to double and when to drop is considered one of the most crucial elements in winning. It is also one of the most important things you need to evaluate during the relationship game. Understanding what to do during the beginning, middle and end of the game, as well as when to drop and cut your losses or stay and increase your risk by moving forward, are personal strategies you need to acquire and utilize. We will describe how many of our survey participants responded to this challenge and give examples of the outcomes of their stay or drop decisions. These strategies can be utilized throughout all three stages of the game: Beginning, Middle and End.

The Casanova-type male will occasionally be referred to in our book. Giancomo Casanova is infamous as a man who truly loved women. He was born in Venice, Italy in 1725 and lived to be seventy-three, which in his era was considered advanced old age. By his account, he made love to more than 130 women. Although he lived almost 300 years ago, his legend continues as a man who constantly sought the company of beautiful women. He treated women with high esteem and respect before, during and after their encounters, and he was obsessed with achieving intimacy with huge numbers of women, each of whom he treated with great respect and confidentiality. This is not an unknown propensity today and we will have some things to say about men with Casanova-like tendencies.

Though Casanova has gained a bad reputation in certain circles over the centuries, it is important to note the high standards of gentlemanly behavior he set for himself, and the utmost respect with which he approached each of his encounters with the women he adored. His drive to bed as many women as possible notwithstanding, many of Casanova's positive qualities are standards to which all men should hold themselves, and women should expect these qualities from their men. So when we refer to Casanova, don't let the alarm bells ring too loudly in your head: he wasn't such a bad guy, after all.

Part I discusses the phases of the Beginning Game. It includes real-life examples, as well as relevant comments from our survey participants, and will point out why the initial date at the beginning level is so crucial. This section will stress the importance of getting out there if you want to find your ideal partner and will also walk you through your first encounters. You will learn who wants what and what both men and women need to do to impress the opposite sex. It will tell you how to position yourself and communicate to your best advantage. Section I will describe what you should look for and what you should avoid in searching for that perfect person through the Internet. And lastly, it deals with the fact that everyone suffers rejection sometime and offers ways to shrug it off and get back in the game. Each dating game true story we recount has a key point about relationship behavior that will provide you with an information database that you can use to find your next great partner.

An interesting event occurred as a result of two people reading the pre-publication version of this book. A woman Mason had dated off and on for around three years got so inspired about applying our rule to get out in the world that she decided it was time for her to meet a man with whom she could have a serious relationship. A man Nancy once dated and who remained a good friend took her advice about all of the good results people were having with Internet dating and signed up with one of the services. He called several weeks later to say he had met a wonderful woman with whom he hoped to develop the kind of relationship about which Nancy and Mason had written. See? Success is possible.

CHAPTER 1

Getting Back in the Game

"Living for the moment is important—don't waste time thinking you can wait a little longer."

Audrey

Deciding to restart your social life after a marriage or long-term relationship ends is a huge step. When you make that decision, you will need to have a workable and realistic plan. Women and men tend to react very differently to starting over. Many men are ready and eager, while a lot of women have a tendency to get into a mode of downtime, where they frequently just don't want to date or even go out—a mode that often can be hard to break. Many women comment that this time of rejuvenation is necessary, especially if the past has consisted primarily of meeting other people's needs for many years.

Once you are ready, how do you begin the dating game? As part of our research, we compiled a lengthy questionnaire, which was completed by more than 400 single, midlife men and women. Of the total responses, 55 percent were from women and 45 percent were from men. When asked, "How important is it to have a great relationship?" 87 percent of men and 85 percent of women stated it was "very important" or "important."

We asked how many times our respondents had been married and received the following responses:

Men:	
never	(13%)
once	(64%)
twice	(22%)
three or more	(1%)

Women:	
never	(12%)
once	(59%)
twice	(26%)
three or more	(3%)

It would seem from these numbers that men and women have essentially the same proclivity for marriage. What seemed somewhat surprising was that the vast majority of both men and women had only been married once and over 10 percent of both sexes had never been married.

It's Time to Make a Plan

The respondents in our study were eager to share how they began the dating game and what has worked best for them. One thing they emphasized was that you need to go to quality places to meet quality people and you need to be *seen*.

When asked where these quality places can be found, they replied:

Men:	
still searching/unknown	(33%)
special interest groups such as hiking, skiing, tennis	(26%)
singles organizations	(19%)
church/church events	(11%)
Internet	(11%)

Women:
still searching/unknown	(31%)
mutual friends	(25%)
special interest groups such as hiking, skiing, tennis	(19%)
singles organizations	(16%)
college reunions	(9%)

The fact that both sexes felt they were still searching for the right place to meet others lends credibility to our point that you really need to get out there if you expect to meet someone. You will not be able to decide one day, "It's time to meet someone," and expect to hear a knock on your front door. It just doesn't happen that way.

The survey also supports the fact that both men and women feel that when they meet others in an atmosphere of common interest and congeniality, they have met potential partners similar to themselves. Thus a relationship can start on the same page and the individuals have a better chance of developing a connection in a much shorter time. Several people who were retired felt the workplace had been a good place to meet people, but now that they did not go to an office, they feel cut off and are trying to tap into their working friends' contacts.

Lots of Options

Many of the respondents in our study recommended a renewed commitment to education—both intellectual and spiritual. Adult education classes, community college seminars, lectures and conferences are all sources they felt would help them grow and become more interesting people. And even if they did not meet anyone especially interesting to date, they had fun, met some new people and learned something.

Others reported they had enrolled in relationship courses, citing "lack of communication" and "immaturity" as two of the key factors in their past relationship breakups. They were determined to have better skills in place to make their next relationship more successful. When asked their goals in taking these classes, the respondents replied: to develop more "tolerance," to learn to "forgive" and to work on being more "intimate."

Waiting For Tomorrow Is Not the Answer

So what else do you do to get back in midlife dating? Even if you can't bring yourself to date immediately after the end of a relationship, you can go out with friends and enjoy social activities. You know that relationships can be what life is all about, but you can't be in another one if you don't make an effort. As one respondent wisely said, "No one is going to pick you out of a crowd in a dark movie theater." Fate can play a role with some assistance. Good men and women are out there, but only if you make yourself accessible will you be able to connect with any of them.

In our modern world, there are numerous sources to assist you in dating: the Internet, personal ads in newspapers or subscribing to one of the many quality personalized dating services. You are able to screen people and focus on finding those with traits you desire in a partner. These fast-growing methods of meeting people are so popular that we have devoted an entire chapter to this subject a little farther on in the book.

The book you are now reading is a good example of the benefits of getting out there. Nancy committed to go to a function to plan a singles party, but on the day of the event she did not feel like going. However, she decided that since she had made a commitment, she should follow through. Mason also was there and mentioned this book. He then said he was looking for a female coauthor. Although Nancy didn't know Mason very well, she felt she would be able to work with him and that there was a definite market for a book on this subject. Chance encounters that lead to good things (maybe even a romance) occur more frequently than one would think.

For most people, it takes considerable time to get back into the social swing of things. Generally, men are far more likely to get back in the dating game quickly. They appear to have more emotional resilience and it often takes them about a nanosecond to start dating after a breakup. They intuitively seem to recognize the need to restart their lives and usually don't waste time thinking about the past—they look to the future. Some women, on the other hand, often take months, and in some cases even years, to get back to a normal social life that includes dating.

Audrey is a fifty-two-year old woman who has had the misfortune to have had three men whom she was dating die, one from a brain tumor, one from a plane crash and the third through a tragic suicide.

These losses taught Audrey one critical lesson: Make every day as productive as you can and don't wait for the next relationship to just drop in your lap. Be proactive in meeting the opposite sex and don't worry about the possibility of rejection in aggressively pursuing someone who interests you. Audrey is a woman who truly loves being in a good relationship and she obviously learned a lesson the hard way. Living for the moment is important, so her advice is, "Don't waste time thinking you can just wait a little longer."

Elizabeth, a single friend of Nancy's, found the love of her life one weekend in Carmel Valley when Nancy invited her to visit for a weekend. A luncheon had been planned by one of Nancy's friends, but Elizabeth said she would rather stay curled up on a couch and read. Nancy insisted she go and she acquiesced. Elizabeth and the host, a retired physician, took one look at each other, were inseparable for several months and married soon after. Elizabeth often says this marriage has been the happiest time of her life. Nancy frequently reminds her that had she not gone to the luncheon she would still be reading relationship books.

Maybe It's Time for a Personal Evaluation

Many respondents in the study stated they used the time after a broken relationship, particularly if it was a lengthy one, to re-engineer themselves. Finding oneself single is a good time to refresh one's physical appearance. Over the years you may have added a few pounds that you rationalized away and didn't do anything about. This is a great time to join a gym or take up other physical activities. One of the best things you can do is to get your body back into reasonable shape.

Women often redo their makeup as well as get a newly updated hairstyle and color. Men, too, might think about a new hairstyle or cut. And unless you have superior skills in matching clothing and accessories, you might want to consider working with a wardrobe consultant at a clothing store or find one who will come to your home. One good rule of thumb is to toss anything you have not worn for at least two years. This job can sometimes be easier if you have the help of a professional standing next to you, helping you decide what stays and what goes. Sentiment or price do not play a role in their judgment. You can even go shopping with the specialist and, while you may pay a little more for your new clothes, they will fit perfectly, last longer and be a great bargain in the end.

Both men and women, particularly if they are retired and staying at home, may have gotten in the habit of wearing dilapidated but comfortable clothing and not paying much attention to their grooming. If this describes you, then it has to stop if you want to get back in the game in a meaningful way. If your goal is to meet someone, you need to pay attention and update your look and your basic attire.

Many of our respondents also recommended going to a dentist to have your teeth checked for yellowing, cracking or chipping. Getting your front teeth in shape can do a world of good for your appearance. Among the many options are whitening them or having porcelain veneers put on, which correct crooked and chipped teeth or gaps between your teeth Whitening is a simple process that is also relatively inexpensive and makes smiling a pleasure. The discoloration of teeth happens gradually and many people get so used to yellowish teeth that they don't realize what a positive difference clean, white teeth make in their appearance.

Patricia, now fifty-eight years old, had been married thirty-three years and had admittedly "let herself go" while raising three children. Upon her divorce she immediately had a neck lift to get rid of her sagging "turkey neck" skin, started going to the gym to lose the twenty pounds she had acquired during the marriage, had her teeth whitened and took up golf as a social sport. Patricia commented that her greatest thrill happened when she ran into her ex-husband, who she had not seen him in two years, in a shopping mall and he exclaimed, "Wow, you look just like you did when we were dating!"

While spending the money necessary for facial surgery or an entire set of front teeth veneers may not be the best choice for everyone, basic attention to getting in shape and getting into new activities is certainly advisable and available to every single one of us. Looking your best often requires a lifestyle change, but the good news is that it is for the better, not only physically, but also emotionally. It will make a difference in how you feel and how you are perceived. Rightly or wrongly, people still put a lot of emphasis on first impressions.

You Don't Get a Second Opportunity to Make a First Impression

Deborah, a fifty-five-year-old career woman who never married, had long been searching for a compatible partner. She commented, "I am smart, I am a businesswoman, I have a great body, I am very sexual—so where are the good men?" A major part of her dilemma was that she worked at home and her business was conducted in distant cities all across the country, making it difficult to meet people or sustain a relationship.

Mason, who is a friend of Deborah's, told her, "You never know where the right man will turn up, maybe even in the airport." Shortly after one of these conversations, Mason had a reason to travel with Deborah on business. She showed up at the airport wearing no makeup, her hair pulled up unattractively, soiled jeans that looked like they had been worn for at least a year without being washed and dirty tennis shoes. Mason asked her "If you want to meet Mr. Wonderful, why do you travel looking like that? No man will be attracted to you if you don't even make an effort to look nice." Her response was, "I just want to be comfortable when I fly across the country."

Deborah may have been comfortable, but the likelihood of meeting an interesting man was an option she was certainly eliminating. You don't need to look like you just stepped out of the pages of a fashion magazine, but you do need to look reasonably presentable when you go out in the world. If you take the time to take care of yourself, you will be surprised at the people you will meet when you least expect it. Many men and women meet each other for the first time in airports, on street corners, at stockholder meetings, in food stores, in business settings and even in waiting rooms of dentists and doctors!

Lisa, a woman in her mid-forties, related the experience of a first date with a man who evidently decided *not* to spiff up for the occasion. She had a date with a successful psychiatrist at local restaurant near her home in Menlo Park, California. He greeted her with a two-day whisker stubble, frayed cuffs on his pants, a 1950s-style plaid sport coat and a baseball cap. During dinner, he spent the entire time proclaiming his great business success, his intention to buy a vacation home in Santa Fe and his desire to meet a woman with whom he could share his life. Most amazingly, after all of this, he proceeded to ask Lisa to pay for half of the dinner! Needless to say, this man did not make Lisa's top ten list. There was no second encounter.

Suzanne tells of meeting a very attractive man in his fifties named Ken at a friend's wedding in Napa Valley. The next week she ran into him at the local drug store. Unfortunately, she was unkempt and wearing an old sweat suit. While he recognized her and said hello, he seemed in a hurry. The next week, Suzanne again saw Ken, this time at the grocery store. She was dressed beautifully in a designer suit, as she had just returned from a business luncheon. Ken was flirtatious. He lingered to talk and, on the spot, asked her out for a date the next week.

Take a Chance

Another scenario of getting back in the game was played out at a party Mason hosted. Sandy, who had been invited, asked if she could bring a friend named Ann. Ann was in a long-term funk about a divorce and did not like the idea of going out and Sandy wanted to give her a reason to be social. She convinced Ann to come to the party where Mason spent a lot of time talking to her and found her to be one of the most attractive and interesting women he had met in a long time. He secured her phone number.

The next morning, Mason received an early call from his friend Ron (at that time a fifty-two-year-old Casanova-type who had never been married). He also had been at the party and met Ann. He similarly found her to be a fantastic woman and told Mason he just had to have her number. Mason told him, yes, he had the number, but *he* was going to take her out—Ron was out of luck.

Well, Ron moaned and groaned about how he really needed to date someone who lived nearby (Ann, he had found out, did), because he was tired of driving to San Francisco for dates. He also told Mason that Ann had a daughter and reminded Mason that he was not very good with young children. Mason found out later that Ann's daughter was in college—Ron conveniently left that out. Finally, since she lived so far from Mason, he should be a good guy and give Ron the first chance to date her. Mason relented and gave him Ann's number. To make a long story short, Ron and Ann got married six months later are living happily ever after.

There are two lessons to be learned here. The first is, as in Ann's case, you never know what may happen when you offer yourself a chance to get out of the house and get back into the social scene. Ann's entire life was changed for the better just because a good friend talked her into going to a party. The second lesson is that Ron, a confirmed bachelor and playboy who had never been married, did so at the age of fifty-two. Once he found the right woman, it took him only six months to make the decision. You constantly women people say, "He hasn't been married, therefore he's a bad risk. Don't waste your time," or "He has a history as a playboy and will never change." Maybe so, but just remember men mature too, and as they do, they tend to want to find permanency in a relationship.

Ron was one of many men who, even though they appear to be wedded to single lives, are, in reality, open to changing their lifestyles. Women need to be aware that while some men take a long time to realize they want permanent relationships, it doesn't mean they never will. Although a surprisingly high percentage (26 percent) of the men in our survey responded, "One," when asked, "How many committed relationships have you had other than marriage?" Nobody said "None."

When men who have been dating for many years finally do enter into exclusive relationships, it is highly likely they are doing so because the women they have chosen are the best of all the women they have previously dated. As they age, men are increasingly likely to be fully committed to their decisions—they have the experience and have dated enough to understand what it is they don't like in a woman. The women they finally choose can be assured that their men know what they want and they have found it.

Get Out There

Another successful example of the advantages of not being reclusive and of getting back in the game is illustrated by Angela's story. A man Angela already knew, who was not going to be her choice for a long-term relationship, invited her to a basketball game, far from her preferred way of spending an evening (but, take note—she went). While there, she met a wonderful man, an acquaintance of her date, who loved her smile, asked for her number and called her the next day to invite her to dinner. Many people in our study commented that they met the loves of their lives when they were out with individuals for whom they did not especially care or while doing something that was not their favorite activity.

Kathleen, who is fifty-eight, met John, moved in with him within one month, became engaged during month two and was married in month three. Absurd, you say? To many, that breakneck pace just seems too fast, but Kathleen's comment was illustrative of a can-do attitude. She said, "When you are older and you meet someone who clicks, you just know it, so why fool around playing games?" Admittedly, Kathleen's experience is not typical, but her attitude is what's important. She recognized that when something feels right between two mature people, there is no reason not to make the move. As she said, "I'm not thirty anymore and here was this great guy. What was I supposed to do, wait until I was seventy?"

There is a caveat to this approach: You must have some knowledge of the history of the person before you move this quickly into a permanent relationship. Kathleen's courtship progressed so rapidly because John had lived in the same area for a long period of time. He had a wide variety of old friends from whom Kathleen learned a great deal about John's past history and admirable qualities. She quickly came to trust him.

Be a Columbo

While it is important to obtain as much information as possible about your date, you need to be circumspect. You might turn your date off if you interrogate him or her in what appears to be a clinical fashion. So be like Detective Columbo on the television series, act naturally, but find out everything you can about this person to whom you're attracted. Anyone who works will have a history, possibly available on the Internet—enter his or her name and address and see what you find. If the individual doesn't want you to know where he or she lives, then take it as a bad sign and move on. Find out what you can without being obvious. It's important to eliminate the person with the Casanova complex (the sexual conquest Casanova—not the gentleman Casanova) who may be at your doorstep and who cannot commit to one person.

Nancy read a letter sent to a newspaper advice column which was, in contrast to Kathleen's experience, an example of how not to find a good mate in a short amount of time. The letter was from a woman we will call Cynthia who, like Kathleen, had married a man after knowing him for only four months. The woman found the man very sincere and charming; he was good with children; he said he did not drink or use drugs; and he had been married once before but had no children. Cynthia eventually discovered that he had five former wives and two children for whom he was not paying child support, as well as several other live-in relationships.

He used Cynthia's credit cards and charged them to the maximum amount possible, forged checks and ran up numerous other joint charge accounts to the limit. He also turned out to have a drug problem and, in a conciliatory move to Cynthia, agreed to go through drug counseling and rehabilitation. He left her after a year and moved in with another woman one week later. Despite his serious faults, he acted like a perfect gentleman, according to Cynthia. However, a little bit of investigation by Cynthia undoubtedly would have exposed his sordid past.

Obviously, there are a couple of lessons here. First, this can happen to men just as easily as it can happen to women. Second, as it says in the articles about detecting fraudulent advertisements, *if it sounds too good to be true, it probably is*. The men and women who prey on the opposite sex in this manner are among the most charming, romantic and charismatic people you will ever meet.

Be Wary of "Too Perfect"

Some people are pros at what they do and they seem like perfect partners. Well, they are perfect—they have honed their skill at taking advantage of others and they play their roles perfectly. In the case of Kathleen, she was protected because she knew John's history (one advantage of being older is that we all have histories that can be checked; in our youth we had only instinct). So what is the answer? You must find out about the person's past—one way or another, by meeting his relatives, talking to his friends (he does have friends, doesn't he?) and asking relevant questions. Use the Internet, credit bureaus, business contacts, etcetera, to obtain as complete a picture as possible.

Granted, since this "perfect person" has just swept you off your feet, it may feel decidedly unromantic to try to check out his or her past. But in the real world, unless you are a foolhardy gambler, you need to know something more detailed about the person other than the fact that he or she is wonderful to be around, attentive, affectionate and good with children.

Self-confidence Is Crucial

The single most important quality both men and women need to display when meeting potential partners is self-confidence, self-confidence, self-confidence. Surveys have shown that both men and women feel confidence is one of the most important and attractive qualities in the opposite sex. Women consider self-confidence to be a very sexy trait in a man, while men consider self-confidence in a woman to be an indication she is self sufficient, poised and not needy. Combine self-confidence with a great smile and you impart a winning attitude that will be attractive to the opposite sex in almost any situation. Our survey participants stressed that they are looking for partners who are happy with themselves, possess serenity and who appear as though they have their lives in good working order.

One cautionary word on one of the most flagrant displays of low self-esteem and lack of self-confidence: When you pass the opposite sex on the street, at work or in your athletic club, *don't look at the ground as you pass him or her by*. It shows a total lack of self-confidence and will insure that you meet no one.

Don't Relive the Past

Relegating all of the negative things about your past relationships to an emotional graveyard is an important start. Nothing positive can happen until you get rid of your bad feelings about what happened yesterday. Don't blame past relationships for what is happening in your life today. Nothing can change history; it is vital that you forget the things that negatively affected you. Once you accomplish this, anything can happen and undoubtedly will.

Let the past be the past, and you will find that the future becomes immeasurably brighter.

Be Realistic

Remember your naïve, uninformed, romantic mental attitude when you married the first time? You were young and very likely had an unrealistic view of what life would be like. The scenario you envisioned might have gone something like this: *We will live in a small apartment, have enough money to go out once a week or so for dinner, buy used furniture, talk about how we will grow together, and work toward the day when we can afford a house and begin our family. In our later years we will have achieved success and be able to travel and live out our lives enjoying our friends and family.* Hopefully, your views have changed and matured because this was a fantasyland, a utopian ideal achieved only by a relatively low number of lucky couples.

The Reality Scenario

Be realistic in your assessment of the person you begin to date and do not be misled by fantasy thoughts. You can match your interests and intellect. Assert yourself and pick the right partner using the rich experience you have gained to avoid the fatal errors of the past. Love at first sight may have been wonderful and exciting, but love at second sight can be even more rewarding, since you have the wisdom that comes with age and the ability to appreciate a world-class relationship.

Are You Ready?

This new midlife adventure can be the best time of your life. Everyone buys the "You're only as young as you feel" line, but let's be honest—the odds are that unless you are terribly lucky and have great genes, you're more likely than not to start to feel (or look) a lot less young after age forty or fifty. Just keep in mind that it helps considerably if you do all you can to improve yourself—physically, intellectually and emotionally. We have a relatively short span of time in this world, so we need to live our lives to the hilt every minute of every day! It's time to develop a new attitude that says, "I'd like to have someone special in my life and I am ready to get back in the game!"

Quiz – Chapter 1

This quick quiz will help you evaluate just how ready you really are to get yourself back into the Dating Game. Please rate yourself:

10 points for a "yes"; 5 points for an "undecided"; 0 points for a "no"

Ranking   Question

_____ 1. I am ready to begin meeting and socializing with people of the opposite sex.

_____ 2. I am starting to get my plan together and I can list the top three places where I can go to meet quality people.

_____ 3. I recently did an in-depth personal inventory of my strengths and weaknesses.

_____ 4. I can list three traits that need improvement and I am willing to work on them.

_____ 5. When I have a date with someone new, I go all out in my appearance, clothes and manners.

_____ 6. I try to be "date smart" and find out all that I can about my date on the first few encounters.

_____ 7. I would rank my self-confidence as high.

Scoring

70 – 60 - You are definitely ready to play the dating game.

50 – 30 - Your appear somewhat tentative—do you really want to get back in the game?

20 – 0 - You may not be ready, but you are not alone. Lots of people are making the same transition.

CHAPTER 2

You Won't Meet People If They Don't Know You're There

"No one is going to simply appear at your front door and say: 'Here I am.'"
Joanne

Remember this simple concept: In order to be discovered, you have to get out and be noticed. This sometimes can be difficult, particularly if you are shy or have lost your social base because of the end of a relationship. Here is a good way to start: First make a list of all the activities you truly enjoy or, alternatively, activities which you wish you could do or know more about. Volunteering for what you consider to be a great cause is a proven way to meet people, whether the cause is political or a non-profit charity. You can also enroll in a course—whether it is bridge, dancing, tennis or a college course. While you are out there you will meet people with similar passions. Even if you don't make a love connection, you will enjoy this time of growth as a gift for yourself!

Be Opportunistic

Carol, a woman in her late forties with whom we met and whose ideas are included in our study, told us, "I try to go where men hang out. I know a lot of men like physical activity, so I go on group hikes, cross-country ski weekends and singles tennis weekends. My best girlfriend met the man of her dreams, Phil, after she went to a professional tennis match. She doesn't particularly like tennis, but a friend dragged her along. She ended up sitting next to Phil and there was instant chemistry. They were very soon in a loving, committed relationship.

Many people of both sexes tend to be shy around one another, despite the myth about aggressive men seeking out women and meeting them in every conceivable circumstance. For example, while many men seem confident and outgoing in other areas of their lives, particularly business, they sometimes are slow or even backward in social situations. Women who become interested in such men may have to overcome their reticence and take the initiative.

It Takes More Than One Encounter

The odds are against you that going on a date with someone new will lead to instant romance. What is a fact, though, is that you will meet a lot of new people who will become good friends, Some will even become lifetime buddies, and they in turn will have other good friends you can meet. The friend of your friend may well be the right one. Many encounters may lead to romance, new job opportunities or other positive life altering situations.

Nancy's friend, Lynn, realized how very lonely she was after two years of being divorced. "Loneliness is the worst part of being single," she told us. She decided to call ten of her friends and ask each of them to get her one date. During the next month she met ten pre-screened people. She clicked with number nine and they married a year later. What's the moral of this story? When you are ready to begin dating, call your friends. Don't hesitate to ask for their help.

Attitude, Attitude, Attitude

There are a few basic requirements in meeting new people. First, have a positive attitude about yourself. Second, have a sense of humor and don't take everything as a serious event in life. Third, and most important, smile and show your self-confidence by making eye contact with others. This lets people know you are open to a conversation.

Many of the women (and a few of the men) interviewed for this book expressed the fact that they have an "anti-aging" philosophy that works for them and could work for a lot of men and women. The strategy is simply the attitude: "I am not getting older." Then pick an age you want to be and act and feel as though it is your age.

Scott is a sixty-two-year old man who is said by his dates to project an attitude of a thirty or forty-year-old, and they love him for it. This playfulness is a key to his meeting new women. One woman who had dated him characterized him as a "sixty-something fun kid." Scott has no trouble attracting women and his youthful attitude is certainly a major reason why.

As most women probably realize, either from experience or just by observing men, the "thinking young" concept is something men mostly do not need to learn. Many men think they are still in their twenties or thirties, regardless of how old they get or how mature they look. In fact, many women have complained over the years that the men in their lives won't grow up.

Unfortunately for men, it's pesky little physical problems like falling testosterone levels, dropping sexual drive, prostate problems and reduced physical endurance that often get in the way of doing everything they did in their younger years. However, even with all of these physical dilemmas stacking up, men should get in the best physical shape possible, maintain an upbeat attitude, get involved in new activities and behave as youthfully as their personalities allow. This is every bit as necessary for men as it is for women.

Sally, a woman in our study who is in her sixties, tells us of returning to her college for an alumni weekend. She had spent the year before doing all she could to improve her appearance. On the first night she sat next to Ben, whom she hardly remembered. During his college years Ben had spent most of his time in the library preparing for law school and had not been very social. He now had a successful practice on Fifth Avenue in New York City and was recently divorced. Ben and Sally immediately hit it off and have had a fabulous relationship for several months. Recently she moved to New York to become his roommate.

When you first meet someone who looks interesting, giving him or her a pleasant smile or a simple "hello" may be all it takes to begin a conversation. Give an indication of your interest, and mild flirting is definitely in order. What's the worst that could happen if you see someone in an elevator, an airport or a restaurant and say, "That's a great outfit" or "That's a great tie?" No response? Rejection?. If that happens, what have you lost? You certainly can recover from a disappointing attempt at flirtation. You can't possibly have a great crisis of self-confidence at this stage of your life over being rejected by some man or woman who doesn't even know who you are! Banish the thought, *I can't do that*. It's time to rethink your attitude, be open to meeting new people and take a chance.

You Never Know Where It Will Happen

Adrian, a forty-seven-year-old businesswoman, met one of the great loves of her life while she was traveling on business in Phoenix. She was sitting at the bar of a restaurant waiting for a table with one of her business associates when one of the best looking men she had ever seen walked into the room. Adrian was positively dazzled and felt meeting him was imperative. While Adrian had little doubt this man would be with another woman, she gathered her courage and boldly walked over to him. Her exact opening line was, "You look familiar to me. Where are you from?" He mentioned a city near where she lives and that was the beginning of a long-term relationship.

The man later mentioned to Adrian that he had also noticed her, but he just didn't feel confident enough to approach her and initiate a conversation. He was very glad she took the initiative, he told her. This illustrates a key point, which is that when it comes to meeting women, most men aren't all that confident. They frequently get even *less* confident as they get older, particularly if they find themselves single after a long marriage or lengthy committed relationship.

Yes, it is true that most men admire women as they move around in their daily life. This doesn't necessarily mean they are able to act and initiate contact.

So ladies, if you catch a man looking at you, it probably means he is interested in you. He may lack the confidence to approach and begin a conversation. Being more aggressive about meeting men, regardless of the circumstance, therefore, is something you should definitely consider. Try Adrian's approach—what have you got to lose? Asking a man for his business card and calling him later is not out of line. And while that may take some courage, you can bet there is a very high probability the man will be delighted you called. If not, you have lost nothing, a rejection is not personal. He doesn't know the real you. It is not a catastrophe, only a minor setback.

The story of Ralph's initiative may pay dividends for constrained men. He is a sixty-three-year-old retired chief financial officer for a large corporation and had been divorced for five years. He was in a restaurant and saw a fascinating-looking woman in a discussion with a friend. Despite his business success, Ralph is relatively shy around women, but he took action that was for him very much out of character. As he said, "This was totally new for me." On impulse, he walked over to the woman and said, "My name is Ralph and I would enjoy meeting you sometime. Here is my business card. I hope you will call me."

Admittedly, this method has a low success rate as a way for a man to meet someone, since women generally do not respond to this approach, but in Ralph's case it worked. The woman called about a week later and they became inseparable companions. She later admitted to Ralph that it was very hard for her to make the call, but her girlfriends urged her on and she finally got up the nerve to do it. Her girlfriends' argument: "What have you got to lose?"

Similarly, Nancy's friend Marge, a highly successful fifty-one-year-old real estate sales representative, went to a cocktail party at a friend's house. She immediately noticed a man she considered extremely attractive. Despite frequent eye contact, he failed to approach her. As she was leaving, she got up her nerve to walk up to him, hand him her card and say, "Call me if you'd be interested in meeting." He called. At last report, they were in their second year of dating. He later admitted to Marge he had been fearful of rejection if he approached her without an introduction during the party. He was happy she took the initiative.

Most Men Are Not "Hunters"

It's important to debunk the stereotypical concept that all men like challenges and will hunt women down and do anything to meet them. Young women may have that perception because they are meeting men in their twenties or thirties who are pretty aggressive (that's why they meet them). While it is true that many men are very active at pursuing women, such men are the most visible precisely because they are so active and, therefore, noticeable. However, these younger men are not indicative of the male population in general.

It's a broad generalization, but we feel safe in saying that at age twenty to thirty, many men like just about any woman who is breathing and looks halfway attractive. This is not as true for older men. Mature men have lives, they do things, they have long-term careers and they aren't nearly as sexually driven as they were when they were younger. They have better things to do at this point in their lives than spend an inordinate amount of time tracking and pursuing women.

This is not to say that middle-aged or older men won't go out of their way to meet women at parties and won't ask for their numbers, but they often won't call back if rejected the first time (unless given a good reason and if interest is expressed in meeting at another time). They also tend not to call again if women don't call them back when they leave a message. Men in a later stage of their lives have figured out that if women are interested, they will call back. If women are playing hard to get by not returning calls, based on some old-fashioned notion that men will continue to pursue them, they will find most men will just forget it and move on.

Be Considerate

Telephone calls have their own etiquette. Women and men both need to remember that in business, one of the worst offenses anyone can make is to not return a phone call—it is considered one of the cardinal sins of business. Everyone in business remembers the people who don't call them back and hopes for the day when the tables are turned and they can "forget" to return calls to those people. This unwritten rule is equally applicable to social situations. If you get a call—return it! You can always make an excuse as to why you can't go out, but the call could mean an invitation to a fun event and someone interesting could be there!

There is one major exception to the call-back rule and women need to be aware of it. There are some men who will continually call you until they make contact and then relentlessly pursue you until they get you to go out with them. These men tend to be controlling, narcissistic, ego-driven men who just can't stand to have *any* woman reject them. They may call multiple times, assuming they can break you down and convince you that you will not regret a date with them. The answer: just say, "No."

A fifty-four-year-old highly eligible bachelor, George, had been fixed up with Ashley and met her for an after-work drink. They had gotten along famously on their first encounter and he called to arrange a second date to see her on a Sunday afternoon. Ashley was very receptive and they made a date. Everything seemed fine, except on Sunday morning when he called to get directions to her house, George discovered she wasn't home. He left a message, but the call was never returned. She did not have the courtesy to say she couldn't make the second date—instead, she stood him up. There was no follow-up call by George. Self-confident men have no need to grovel for dates and most will not follow up what they perceive to be gamesmanship.

Whether Ashley was playing hard to get or she had some other agenda is almost incidental. Her behavior was discourteous. Think about it. Why would a man demean himself by continually calling a woman who did not return calls? Why would a woman want a man who thought so little of himself as he would after receiving such treatment? Secure and successful men and women have better things to do.

There are any number of potential consequences for such rudeness. The rejected caller may make disparaging comments about the other person's manners and sense of etiquette to others and cause him or her social problems elsewhere.

Be Open and Observant

Camille was waiting for a blind date named Nick in a charming Chicago trattoria. It was a great place to eat and there were a lot of people arriving for dinner. Her date was very late (which, incidentally, Camille took as a bad sign and so should you). While she anxiously waited, she casually made eye contact with a number of men as they walked by, asking, "Are you Nick?"

A few men responded with, "I wish I were" and it was apparent to Camille that with some encouragement, a number of men would have readily continued to banter with her. That gave Camille a great idea. She commented in our survey that now when she wants to meet someone, she just walks up to him and says "Are you Nick?" Try it!

A slight variation on this meeting scenario occurred several years ago when Carrie had a blind date with a man named Dave at a San Francisco restaurant on a Friday night. As she entered the front door, a man caught her eye and smiled. She just presumed it was Dave looking for her. She walked over to him and said, "Hi, I'm Carrie, are you Dave?" He nodded and after a few words they proceeded to a table for dinner.

Carrie became completely smitten by Dave and it seemed mutual. They spent the entire dinner laughing and sharing things in common, a classic "instant chemistry" meeting. Well, fast forward to the conclusion of the evening: Carrie and Dave spent the night together at her house. In the morning "Dave" looked at Carrie and said, "I have a confession to make, I'm not Dave."

Of course, by this time, that was an incidental issue, because the initial assumption that this "Dave" was her date had led to a wonderful evening. This harmless deception had a happy ending. Carrie eventually married "Dave" and they have lived together happily for the past ten years. It is an example of what can happen when you are willing to take risks in saying hello to a new person. So the next time you are out and you see someone interesting, just say, "Hi, are you Dave" or "Hi, are you Carrie" (it works for men too) and see what happens. It really won't hurt and you may be pleasantly surprised.

Make It Easy to Be "Found"

Something many non-working men and women may not think of, but which is important, is that everyone should have business cards. You can simply have your name and phone number printed on a white, business-size calling card. One of the great dilemmas men often face in asking for a woman's phone number is not having a paper and pen handy. This, of course, is something men can remedy—they should always have a pen available. But even when they do, in particular situations, it is often not convenient or it is awkward to write down a name and number.

For women, having a card will not be perceived by men to be aggressive or desperate; it merely appears organized and professional. So make it easy! People who are retired from business often print business cards, just as a matter of course, since they are used to the process of handing out cards when they meet new people. They know it is a simple way to interact with others who perhaps will want to contact them. Most stationary stores print cards for a reasonable rate and will even give you design and color options. One caveat: Some individuals, even though they ask for a phone number or card, will not call. It's just one of those things that happens, so don't be disappointed if the phone doesn't ring. Shrug it off and move on.

Make Logical Decisions

Ruth is a woman in her fifties who consistently amazes her friends with her ability to meet men. She has a very open and pleasing personality, but she also puts herself in situations where she can meet people. One of the things she does is attend the stockholder meetings of large corporations in her area (you need to be a stockholder, but any number of shares qualify—even one). She met Philip, who was also attending one of the meetings. They had a three-year relationship that only ended after she made the decision to drop him, (remember the "stay" and "drop" option) when she concluded he was not going to make her a permanent part of his life (incidentally, Philip was eight years younger than Ruth—a topic covered later in this book). How she came to the conclusion to drop Philip is actually a very good lesson in "reading" your potential partner.

During the course of their relationship, Ruth and Philip had many discussions about buying a vacation home together. One night after dinner, Philip casually mentioned he was buying a vacation home with his sister in exactly the same place he and Ruth had discussed buying. To Ruth this was an immediate red flag. It seemed appropriate to conclude that Philip was not considering her in his long-term planning.

She immediately challenged him and asked why he would do that when they had essentially agreed to buy something together. He vacillated and stammered, saying this was just a stopgap plan, certainly he and Ruth would buy something the next year. Ruth realized he was unable to commit and made the decision to end the relationship.

You can debate the haste of her decision or whether she should have made it at all and perhaps she should have just stayed in the Game to see what played out. Maybe she should not have made such an important decision so quickly without pondering or otherwise discussing the ramifications of this decision with Philip in more depth. However, she decided to take action rather than wait another few months, becoming more and more involved. After all, one of the basic themes of this book emphasizes, waiting is a luxury you no longer have in your mid-years as you did in your twenties and thirties.

Be Approachable

As fate would have it, and helped by Ruth's ability to be open and friendly to personal encounters, another man appeared in her life. This occurred only two months after she had broken it off with Philip. Bruce was shopping in a grocery store and was buying a bottle of drinking water. He noticed Ruth next to him in the checkout line with a bag of chocolate chip cookies. He looked at her and said, "Hi, my name is Bruce. Do you want some water to go with those cookies?"

She decided he seemed interesting and thought the approach was novel so she said, "I'm Ruth and sure, why not?" They walked out of the store eating cookies and drinking water and now they are engaged to be married. Bruce, incidentally, is a sixty-five-year-old man who was divorced after a thirty-year marriage. When asked how he got the nerve to talk to Ruth, he said, "She just looked approachable. I really can't believe I did it! I hadn't approached a woman in thirty-two years, but I'm glad I did."

Men's Rules of Encounter

Men need to get over their fears (as Bruce did) of talking to attractive women they may encounter in unexpected places. There are, admittedly, only a limited number of great things you can do if you see a woman who looks interesting, but there are three specific things you *should not do* in trying to meet new women.

1. If you see a woman who looks like someone you know or looks like a movie star or television personality—*do not* say to her, "You look like my sister" or "You look like Goldie Hawn" (or another famous personality). Most women do not believe the comment and perceive it to be a weak and unimaginative attempt to strike up a conversation.

2. If you happen to get in a conversation with a woman and decide to ask for her phone number or to be even more forward and ask her out on the spot, be sure you do it with a sense of confidence and with a tone that lets her know you are really interested in taking her out. Don't say, "Well, maybe we should go out if you ever have any free time" or "I would like to take you out, if you're not too busy." These statements do not project self-confidence. Just ask, "How would you like to go out to dinner Saturday?" or "May I have your phone number? I'd like to ask you out." Since most women are attracted to confident men, the more positive approach will increase your odds of success.

3. The use of basically inane comments or questions like, "Do you like to dance?" or "Do you like to listen to music?" didn't work when you were thirty and certainly won't work now that you are older. They just move you that much farther down the ladder of success. Actually, comments like, "Haven't I met you somewhere?" aren't all that bad. Remember, it worked for Adrian in the airport.

So what should you say? Believe it or not, a simple, "Hi, I'm Jack. How are you doing tonight?" is a pretty good opener. It is simple and shows you have the confidence to just say, "Here I am." Or offer a simple compliment on a woman's clothes or her jewelry or hairdo as an opening gambit to a conversation—something sincere, like, "That's a great dress." If she is interested, she will respond and you will be in the game.

Hanna, a forty-nine-year-old schoolteacher, met her fiancée at a gas station. According to her, as she was ready to pump her gas, a highly attractive man pulled up behind her. Thinking quickly, Hanna asked him for help in operating the pump. After a lively conversation, he then asked her to lunch and the rest, as they say, is history!

Another interesting approach given the new world of E-mail is to say to a woman, "I would be interested in chatting with you sometime. Why don't you give me your E-mail address?" If you can come up with something humorous or witty, all the better. Most women love a humorous attitude and they make it a high priority when composing their mental lists of things they like in a man.

Keep an Open Mind

Women should keep in mind that since most men are not exactly professionals at approaching women (and who would want a professional?), they may make comments or use opening lines that sound dumb or unpolished. Don't arbitrarily reject a man who does this; he is probably just nervous. If he appears to be attractive to you otherwise, make a humorous comment like, "Is that the best you can do?" or anything else that comes to mind that will give him another chance to speak. If he seems interesting to you, just be sure you do respond—say *something*.

The key for both men and women is that there is absolutely nothing to lose by being open and outgoing toward the opposite sex as you go through your daily activities. The *approach* you use is not really important, but if you want to begin to have a new and different life that includes a partner, you will need to do something about it. You need to be proactive, whether that means making new friends, finding new activities or changing your physical appearance. Ruth, the woman mentioned earlier with the outgoing attitude, has a motto she abides by: "Assume good intentions from the opposite sex and live life fully."

Take Time to Look Presentable

An interesting lesson was learned by Betty, a fifty-five-year-old writer of short stories. She was very religious, attended church on a regular basis and had gotten in the habit of getting up to attend early morning mass. Since she was in a hurry, she did not stop to put on makeup or put on anything other than very casual clothes. Some months later she had a discussion with a male friend who also attended mass at the same times she did. His comment was that he really felt sorry for her because she looked so bedraggled and unhappy.

He then proceeded to say that he had seen her at a social event when she was dressed up and wearing makeup, and was astounded by how good she looked. He said to her, "I had no idea you could look so great!"

Clearly, it's very easy for both genders to fall into a pattern like this and get lazy about their physical appearances. But just keep in mind that you never know when a member of the opposite sex may be in the vicinity and ignores you because of your appearance. Most people, after all, are not attracted to a bedraggled look.

Networking Is Important

One woman in our study, Phyllis, a sixty-four-year-old retiree and, by her definition, a professional volunteer, is having great success meeting interesting people. Four days a week she goes "to work"—one day at a hospital, one day at her state senator's local office, one at the foreign students' office at a nearby university and one at her church. She went from being married for thirty-five years to being a divorced woman with no single friends to having a network of over fifty remarkable people. She has a full social life that includes meeting a variety of interesting men.

Meeting people is not a simple process. Meeting the right person for a permanent partnership is analogous to a business process. You cannot just throw up your hands and say, "There are no good men to be found," or "I meet only embittered, cynical women when I go out." This negative kind of mindset is simply self-defeating. If entrepreneurs had this give-up attitude every time they were rejected by the literally hundreds of potential investors who did not see their visions of the future, they would find themselves in the unhappy situation of simply working for someone else just to survive.

Granted, everyone does not have an entrepreneurial attitude, but if you want to do more than just survive, perseverance is necessary. The parallels to business in the social world are clear, and as hard as it may seem, getting in front of new people is the only way to find your next partner. Business and dating situations require perseverance. What person in business do you know who has succeeded by saying, "I can't do that?"

Don't Get Discouraged

Remember this rule: Don't let bad timing or minor setbacks stop you from continuing toward your goal. True, you may need to adapt as your situation changes, but getting discouraged and giving up is not the answer. Keep your spirits high and remember, as Joanne told us, "No one is going to simply appear at your front door and say, 'Here I am.'"

Make an effort to put yourself in situations where you may meet interesting people. This can be any number of places: church socials, classes, university affiliated activities, book clubs or outdoor oriented organizations. Volunteer for what you consider worthwhile causes. Accept invitations even if they are not your ideal venue or from the ideal person, because you never know when the person you are looking for will be there looking for you! Adopt the attitude that says, "Today could be it." Look your best, keep your eyes open and be ready to meet the love of your life.

Quiz – Chapter 2

Are you really ready to make an effort to venture forth and meet new people? This quick quiz will help you evaluate just how ready you really are. Please rate yourself:

10 points for a "yes"; 5 points for an "undecided"; 0 points for a "no"

Ranking   Question

_____ 1. I am currently volunteering for a worthwhile cause.

_____ 2. I am currently enrolled in a class of some kind.

_____ 3. I would accept an invitation from someone I was not especially fond of with the hope of meeting someone new.

_____ 4. I have called (or will call) a friend and asked to be fixed up with one of his or her friends.

_____ 5. I have an open attitude about meeting new people; I try to look approachable.

_____ 6. I would go up to an attractive stranger of the opposite sex (in the right circumstance)and say "hello."

_____ 7. I am beginning to acquire a large number of acquaintances for new social opportunities.

Scoring

70 – 60 - You are definitely willing to try to meet someone interesting. All it takes now is a little luck and good timing.

50 – 30 - You are undecided. But you are becoming aware that it is time to let yourself be discovered.

20 – 0 - Begin to build outside contacts. It isn't that difficult—you just need to make an effort and do it!

CHAPTER 3

Who Wants What

"When I was in my twenties, I did not realize the lasting power
of a companionable relationship."

Chad

Our research points out that mature men and women seek distinct characteristics from the opposite sex in a relationship. However, most of our survey respondents have realistic expectations. Unlike many people in their twenties who have fanciful wish lists, the midlife crowd is willing to make certain adjustments and understands these are often necessary. The qualities they look for today often are much different than those which were sought in early adulthood. Instead of making lists for Santa and expecting it all, they are willing to make compromises. The key is *what* compromises they're willing to agree to.

Men Have Changed

According to our study, midlife men state they are looking for a woman who has the following attributes:

common interests	(34%)
attractive	(22%)
intelligent and educated	(17%)
romantic and sexual	(13%)
fun and into a lot of activities	(9%)
someone who can support herself	(5%)

Explaining his vote for "common interests" as his number one goal in a potential mate, forty-nine-year-old Chad told us, "I no longer look for the homecoming queen—what really matters now is how well she can enjoy herself and relate to me. When I was in my twenties, I did not realize the lasting power of a companionable relationship."

The fact that "someone who can support herself" even appears on the list is undoubtedly due to the fact that many men have lost significant financial resources through divorce (and do not want to go through that painful process again) and now want women who have the ability to take care of themselves financially. This also indicates some men are not good candidates for women who are looking for financial salvation. Equally significant is the fact that "attractive" stays near the top—clearly men have not lost their appreciation for attractive women. This reinforces our contention that new entrants in the midlife dating game must make every effort to present the most appealing look possible.

Our male respondents further told us that when they were younger, they looked for these attributes:

attractive, social, fit	(40%)
sexually appealing	(21%)
similar background	(16%)
family oriented	(13%)
educated and intelligent	(10%)

Of significance is the fact that "sexual" moves from number two on the list of what men wanted in their younger years to number four today, and the concept of "romance" also becomes more prominent, something not often uppermost in the minds of younger men. One man said, "I looked for corporate acceptability, fiscal conservatism and social management in a potential marital partner when I was young. No wonder my first marriage didn't work—it sounds like I was looking for someone to go into business with."

"Family oriented" drops off the chart as a trait desired by men as they get older. It appears that men have had their fill of the obligations of family and want to enjoy life with a partner. And there is good news for smart women! Intelligence as a desired attribute moves up the ladder from

10 percent when men were younger to 17 percent today. That shows men are at least making some progress as they age.

Women Have Gotten More Sexual

The women in our study report that now that they are in their middle years the key attributes they look for in a man are:

romantic and sexual	(36%)
educated and intelligent	(28%)
financially secure	(19%)
sense of humor	(8%)
spiritually aware	(6%)
loyal and thoughtful	(3%)

The women stated when they were *younger* and looking for a mate, they wanted:

potential to be a good provider	(30%)
educated and intelligent	(25%)
good companion	(16%)
romantic and sexual	(15%)
qualities for a good father	(13%)
adventuresome, kind and fun	(1%)

Note that potential to be a good provider becomes "financially secure" and also drops to third on the wish list of mature women. Only "educated and intelligent" and "romantic and sexual" remain on the list of the qualities women now want.

Interestingly, "romance and sexuality," coupled at 36 percent, indicates that mature women have become more like younger men in their view of sex. This romantic requirement also clearly indicates a desire for someone who is sexually aware. Even more surprising, this attribute moved into the number one requirement for older women, while older men moved it *down* to number four. As with men, family-oriented issues seem to disappear for older women. "Qualities for a good father" becomes a non-factor and "spiritual" now comes into play with 6 percent of women wanting this quality in a mate. Those looking for "financial security" (19 percent) may be women who did not work outside the home during their marriages, and now find themselves somewhat economically deprived or concerned about their financial futures. Some may be women who are financially secure themselves and do not want the economic responsibility of taking care of a new partner.

Another point discussed by many participants during our interviews that was interesting, although not statistically significant, was that both women and men indicated it was more important that they both have a good relationship with *her* children rather than *his*. This was a surprising concept, especially since men agreed it was the women's children who were the most important to their overall relationships. This may be due to the fact that often divorced men's children lived with their mothers, sometimes at great distances, and they were not a part of the men's day-to-day lives.

Given the fact that women prize loyalty (number six), it is important for men to tread carefully when divulging past infidelities (i.e. "I had two affairs while I was married"). This is an egregious error that will immediately move a man to the bottom of a woman's list. Men also should avoid any comments that make them appear unethical or untrustworthy in any way. During conversations, if men appear secretive or evasive, most women will get the impression they have something to hide. Mature women are not likely to be intrigued by mysterious sounding men. If anything, they will instantly be wary.

The ability to be thoughtful, also a top-six pick of midlife women is very important and is illustrated well by Mindy's story. Due to circumstances beyond her control, she arrived at the restaurant where she was to meet her date thirty minutes late. Of course, she felt badly and immediately began to apologize, but her date interrupted by giving her a hug and saying, "A beautiful woman like you is well worth the wait." This gesture not only put her immediately at ease, but also put a very large plus in her mind next to this man's name in the category of male thoughtfulness. Mindy did not reveal the outcome of the date, but clearly this man was off to a great start.

Honesty Is a Magnet

Clarence, a fifty-five-year-old man divorced after fifteen years of marriage, was a master at communication and he didn't even know it. After a couple of drinks, Clarence would loosen up and get very philosophical about the "meaning of life." He would stay up until dawn telling his dates his life story and what he felt about everything from nature to marriage. Clarence told his close friend Frank about these encounters and how with few exceptions, the women responded very positively and seemed to become unbelievably attached to him even in a very short period of time.

How was this possible? Frank wondered. Why weren't these women walking away, shaking their heads and wondering where the sane men were? Frank finally figured it out. Most women rarely had the experience of a man opening up his entire life to them and talking without restraint. Not only did Clarence stay up with them until dawn pouring out his soul, but he asked them what their inner feelings were, listened carefully to their responses and never made a sexual move. This display of total honesty and interest in their inner being, coupled with sexual restraint, was an irresistible combination! And Clarence didn't even realize what he was doing—he was just being himself.

Significantly, both genders gave highest marks to attributes other than looks. "Handsome good looks" are not in demand by most mature women to the degree they might have been when they were younger. Instead women look for the self-assurance that comes from success and power in the professional world or from an innate self-confidence. Most men, it must be noted, do not put "a good body" at the top of their list, looking instead for companionship, style and social competence.

Some Men's Body Bias

Although not a survey question, it is worth mentioning the partiality some men have for women with slim or curvaceous bodies. Women have heard this from men for years. And it is a fact that these men will not even consider dating a woman unless she has big breasts, long legs or whatever else they find irresistible—an admittedly immature attitude, but it exists.

Machismo-affected comments by men pertaining to the fact that they met a great gal, but "she doesn't have any breasts" obviously implies that because of this "flaw" she is less than perfect. When this happens other men may tend to nod agreement even if they don't agree with that point of view. However, if you are a woman who doesn't meet these immature standards, and you encounter one of these men, know that because of his body bias, he may not call you even though you assumed you mutually liked one another.

Although there is no way to know if that is why the man is not calling, be advised that this may be the reason. It's totally illogical, but not for these men. This is just another reason not to give even a nanosecond of thought as to why a particular man doesn't call.

Traits Women Dislike

Very high on women's list of dislikes are the men who "talk down" to them. These men will subtlety cast doubt on women who profess success or knowledge in any endeavor or specific subject and will generally display a condescending manner towards them. Sometimes men are not even aware they do this and it may be a habit that just evolved during their adulthood. Men who find they are consistently rejected after their first dates, seemingly for no reason, might consider whether or not this is one of the problems. Today, there is little tolerance of men who demean women's success or independence.

Another issue for many women is men's big rush to have sex. This is a standard complaint women seem to have had since the beginning of time. And it still persists. Most women in midlife have a very strong tendency to reject early sexual moves and are put off by men who try to make sexual moves too fast. What is truly amazing to many women as they told us during our interviews, is that men will often try to make sexual approaches even when it seems evident to the woman they are not even compatible! While the majority of men have learned that fast moves generally are not the way to women's hearts, many still have Neanderthal tendencies.

Men may take physical approaches to their dates based solely on the fact that *they* have chemistry for the women without considering the possibility or recognizing that the women don't have the slightest interest in them. This is a case of simply failing to read the signs. Such men usually have a consistent failure rate with women, because they have little basic respect for women's needs or points of view.

For those men who had success with women in their youth and believe women are now going to want them just because they are single and breathing—think again. Men should make a sexual approach to women only when they get some indication the woman is interested! Men, you can learn to read the signs. Good indicators are simply to touch the woman's arm in a restaurant or put your arm around her when walking to the car (after the date, not before). If she stiffens or moves away, you have a pretty good indication that she is not yet ready to take their relationship to the next level.

Looks Are Often Overrated

Our study indicated that many women are not overly concerned about a man's physical appearance. They often put physical attributes (looks and weight) much lower than self-confidence, honesty and humor on their list of desirable qualities. Casanova was a perfect example of charm trumping good looks in women's eyes. He had a very large nose, a bloated face and receding hairline—a totally unattractive man by classic standards. He was not rich or from the upper class. Yet his legend as a man who won sexual favors from women of all walks of life—aristocratic women, actresses and even fanatically religious women—has persisted.

How did this happen? According to his writings, he was able to accomplish these feats of seduction because he dressed impeccably, he was considerate, gallant and charming, he projected confidence and was constantly attentive to each woman's needs and interested in what she had to say. Given the widely known penchant of Casanova to offer chocolate during the process of seducing a woman, we can also conclude he was clearly ahead of his time in understanding the value of this particular confection. While it was known that Casanova rarely stayed around after seducing a woman, this did not negate the value of his ability to charm and captivate a woman.

Stuart, a relatively unsuccessful sixty-four-year-old man living in Phoenix, is a classic example of this phenomenon. He is quite stocky and balding—yet he constantly finds new women to date solely based on his impeccable clothing, wit, charm and humor. Stuart is a living example of how men who lack good looks, a fit body or financial success can easily meet and date suitable women. For men, working on the charm factor will greatly increase the odds that women will respond positively to their advances. How often have we seen an unattractive man walking down the street with a gorgeous woman and wondered how that happened? It's not always about money. Very often it's due to the fact that the man is pleasant and gallant. Almost all women find simple manners and a gentlemanly attitude very compelling attributes.

Try a Chivalrous Approach

Arlene is a woman who travels in the upper classes of society. She is fifty-three-years-old, looks great and has homes in San Francisco, New York and Paris. Her major complaint about the men she meets is, "They lack knowledge of basic manners and don't know how to be gentlemen. If I found a man I could take to a restaurant who had the skills to make simple gestures like hold my chair while I was being seated, stand when I introduced him to a friend, not put his elbows on the table and, last but not least, not pretend to be a wine expert by doing something like sniffing the cork when it is removed by the waiter, I would be ecstatic." Clearly, Arlene is resorting to a bit of hyperbole, but she obviously places a high value on a man's social behavior, decorum and attentions.

Men who know how to be gentlemen, project honesty and confidence and have a sense of humor, will, just as Casanova did, find no shortage of women. A woman's definition of chemistry is frequently not a physical reaction, but a response to some other good quality she perceives in a man. Men who recognize this will always find success.

High-maintenance Is Not All about Money

Men, too, have their complaints about the opposite sex. Not surprisingly, they are different than women's laments. From our interviews we learned that the qualities high on many men's lists of "can't stands" in a woman are negative or high-maintenance attitudes. In these examples, "high maintenance" refers to the emotional aspect, not the financial. A consistently heard comment from some men who are divorced is that their former wives evolved into constant complainers who could never be satisfied.

Al gave us an example of this type of behavior when he told us about a recent trip to the grocery store. The woman in front of him had four small items she was purchasing. She made a big issue about putting the items in different bags, proceeded to write a check for the amount (which was under five dollars) and then complained the clerk had gotten a small amount of water on one of the paper bags. As she left, she made the parting comment that the service she received was intolerable and she probably wouldn't return to the store.

Al commented to the male clerk "Well, it could be worse, you could be married to her." The clerk responded, "I would last about a minute being married to her." The man in back of Al, who had overheard all of this, said, "I would last about ten seconds." Al then commented that since he was older and far mellower, he could have tolerated her attitude for at least two minutes. The moral of this story is that no one likes complaining, negative people. These qualities are not indicative of a happy person and will cause most men to have second thoughts about any type of follow-up date, much less a relationship.

Another example of high maintenance behavior was exhibited by a first date Marco, a software company president, had last year. Marco is forty-eight years old and, while he is very successful, he is not pretentious. He took his date to a relatively new restaurant he knew would be crowded, but which he also knew had walk-in seating. The restaurant was more crowded than usual and the only seating was at the counter (with a view into the kitchen, which many of the better restaurants now offer), so he suggested they sit there. His date looked at him in shock and said, "I would never sit at a counter." Most men will take this not only as a sign of a total lack of flexibility, but a major indication of an intractable attitude. This might not be considered "high maintenance" to everyone, but to some men it would be reason enough not to call again.

The Mystery of Chemistry

While most women would say knowing the inner person is more important, physical attractiveness still tends to be very high on many men's list of qualities that must be present before they'll ask a woman out on a date. Although it is a trait most women would call shallow, many men are driven by physical attractiveness, in fact that would probably be their definition of chemistry. As much as women dislike this, it's a male characteristic that is probably not going to change.

The good news is that as men move into the midlife of dating the vast majority of them do begin to mature and value women more for their compatibility quotient than for their physical attributes. Many of the men who in their twenties and thirties had to have physical perfection in women now have grown up and learned there are other more important factors in relationships.

Of course, individuals who are not physically appealing on the initial date will not have a follow-up date no matter what potential connection they may have felt existed. This does not mean all men and women must have perfect bodies and looks to attract the opposite sex. It just means that some individuals place more importance on appearances and want partners who are appealing to *them* and fall within *their* definition of desirable. It does not mean you need a rock-solid body or stunning looks to attract others; it just means you have encountered a roadblock with that particular person. Don't be discouraged if you encounter this situation and someone you thought you'd like to see again doesn't feel the same. Few people succeed with any endeavor on the first few tries and dating is no different.

To increase the chances of achieving chemistry based on looks, both men and women should work at getting in the best physical shape possible. This will work wonders for health-related issues as well. Acquire a basic wardrobe that is up-to-date, youthful, but not based on a fad and flattering. Invest in a good haircut and styling and, perhaps, a new color. Good grooming is a must for any age and professionally manicured hands and feet are not only for women these days. Smooth, moisturized skin is tactily alluring for both men and women. Why else would there be such a vast array of male skin care products on the market?

No matter what your body looks like, if you think you may find yourself in a situation in which your clothing is shed, attractive under garments that are becoming to your body type will be a turn on for your partner. Women wearing lacy lingerie are not only a turn on for men but they will probably feel sexier and more desirable themselves. Attention to such matters is important to women as well. One woman in our study told us, "For me, the sexiest sight in the world is a man in pressed, silk pajamas, looking like he just got of the shower and smelling subtly of cologne."

Other Enhancements

Just remember, however, appearance only gets you in the door. It will not take the place of a knowledgeable, upbeat, self-assured, personality. We all gravitate toward people who possess positive attitudes and dress to project style and self-assurance. If you display these qualities and create an interesting, energetic aura about yourself, you will have no problem meeting and dating interesting people.

Here are two examples of physically non-perfect individuals who use their other attributes to attract partners. One of our interviewees, Alex, recently had a discussion with his friend Vincent about the new woman in Vincent's life. With dubious tact, Alex had noted that the lady was rather overweight. Vincent agreed, but said that she was still reasonably fit and active despite the extra pounds.

More importantly, however, she had a delightful way about her and a lively intellect. She dressed attractively, was impeccably well-groomed, and, well, he just liked her a lot. "Why would I let a less-than-perfect body prevent me from dating such a lovely woman?" he asked.

The somewhat amazing irony, of course, is that some men say, "I only want to date a well-proportioned or a thin woman," but don't have any compunction about being overweight themselves. If you ask this type of man, who is clearly overweight or out of shape, if he thinks he can still get a woman with a perfect body, he will just say, "Sure I can." It's as though his own inability to stay fit has no bearing on the issue. Men learn as they get older that, in fact, they can let their bodies turn to flab and still attract women. This, of course, is even more true for men who have mastered Casanova's techniques of being as charming, flattering and respectful to women as they can. This also is validated by our survey that showed most women do not place physical attractiveness in their top list of must haves.

Robin is in his early sixties and has such a large stomach that he can't bend over. It has been commented by others that he looks like he is pregnant with quintuplets. Men at the tennis club to which Mason and he belong have facetiously commented that it would be impossible for Robin to have sex as there is no way his stomach would let him get close enough to a woman to consummate the act.

Yet, to the amazement of everyone, Robin's innate charm, sense of humor and down to earth, self-deprecating acceptance of his immense belly consistently enable him to find attractive women who will go out with him. Since Robin also adheres to the gentlemanly rule of not discussing the particulars of his dates, no one knows if he ever has sex, but his friends suspect he somehow has figured out a way.

Keep It Simple to Start

A situation in which men and women often become nervous is when relatively new romantic partners push too hard and too fast to introduce them into every segment of their lives, such as introducing them to their children, siblings, parents and every friend they have had since grade school. Bringing family and friends into the relationship too early can potentially present a whole new set of problems—it is best to have a more solid foundation before dealing with these types of issues. And while there may not be children living at home, just remember the rule applies to grandchildren, too. The beginning of a relationship is the time to get acquainted and have fun. It is also probably better to spend time alone together in the first few weeks of the relationship—not with family or friends. The pressures of dealing with the scrutiny of unfamiliar people do not evoke romantic fantasies for most people, especially men. Anyway, what's the rush?

Introducing adult children living at home, however, is another matter. After a couple of dates, it is perfectly acceptable to let them meet the candidate. This is actually a good idea, because if you are willing to accept your older children's judgment, they often prove to be very intuitive and may give you some valuable insights on the new person in your life. The key is you have to be willing to listen to what they have to say, even if it's not what you want to hear!

Do You Fit the Criteria?

Let's review the key personality qualities men and women find most desirable according to our survey. Men are seeking someone with whom they feel a commonality of interests, who is attractive, intelligent and has a positive attitude. They also want a woman who is self-confident and has an awareness of the world around them. A low-maintenance demeanor is high on most men's lists. Men rarely are attracted to those who project a complaining or highly competitive image. Those women who are overly assertive, a trait not to be confused with self-confidence, may be seen as argumentative, something that neither gender finds attractive.

Men are highly attracted to an open, happy attitude. Our male interviewees said that they will go to great lengths to avoid women who appear to be in need of excessive emotional assistance or have negative attitudes.

Women reported they are looking for a loyal friend and men who are educated, intelligent and financially secure. They want men who have learned (or not forgotten) the art of romance and who possess a sense of humor. Women definitely want men who will be attentive to them. Just listening to and valuing the woman's opinion will often carry the day for a man, since many women have been in relationships in which they felt ignored. Two-way communication is a key ingredient for friendship and men who have taken women for granted in the past and continue to do so will find far less success in the midlife dating game than they may have enjoyed in their youth.

Closer to Agreement

Our study clearly shows that as men and women mature they seek more of the same attributes in a relationship than when they were younger. Both sexes seek friendship and a sense of common interests. In our discussions with respondents they all emphasized that they wanted partners who had taken care of themselves both physically and emotionally. Most of us who have achieved our middle years have had the life experiences that allow us to be the *real* people the opposite sex are seeking for those special relationships.

The best and most humorous analysis of changing attitudes of both men and women as they advance into age is best illustrated by a story we received from Rae and Landon, two of our survey respondents. They live next door to each other and have been friends for over fifty years.

This is how Rae responded to the question of what she wanted in a man: "When I was fifty, I looked for a man who was handsome, financially successful, in good shape and who dressed with style. When I was sixty, I looked for a man who was nice looking (preferably with hair on head), had enough money for a good dinner, carried bags of groceries with ease and owned at least one silk tie. When I turned seventy, I looked for a man with facial skin who was not too damaged by the sun (being bald was now acceptable), splurged on going out for dinner occasionally, was in good enough shape to slide furniture across the room and wore a shirt that covered his stomach. Now that I am eighty, I want a man who keeps his nose and ear hairs trimmed, doesn't borrow money too often, is in good enough shape to get off the couch under his own power at the end of the evening and usually wears matching socks."

Landon told us: "When I was fifty, I wanted a woman who was a good listener and charming, who appreciated the finer things and was an imaginative, exciting lover. When I turned sixty, I looked for someone who laughed at my jokes, who knew not to buy jug wine with a screw top, listened more than she talked and enjoyed taking part in sex at least once a week. When I was seventy, I sought a woman who didn't doze off when I talked, could walk to the car under her own power when we went out, appreciated a good TV dinner and remembered when it was the weekend. Now that I am eighty, I am hopeful of finding a woman who knows where she left her hearing aid, can still drive a car and doesn't drive off until I am in it, would consider having sex once a month and doesn't snore too loudly."

Quiz – Chapter 3

Do you understand what men and women want in midlife? This quick quiz will help you evaluate your comprehension of the differences. Please rate yourself:

10 points for a "yes"; 5 points for an "undecided"; 0 points for a "no"

Ranking   Question
_____ 1. I can list three attributes that men (or women) want.
_____ 2. I am looking for more mature and long-lasting qualities than I did when I was in my twenties.
_____ 3. I understand the differences between economical and emotional high maintenance and I try not to be either.
_____ 4. I make the maximum effort to have a good appearance.
_____ 5. I would have a second date with someone even though I felt there was no instant chemistry.
_____ 6. I let some time go by before bringing my date into my circle of friends or family.
_____ 7. I can support myself and I do not want to be used as a meal ticket.

Scoring

70 – 60 - You are being successful in your attempts to be social. You definitely know how to play the Beginning Game.
50 – 30 - Sounds like you are somewhat undecided or unsure how to proceed.
20 – 0 - Maybe you need to jump start your social life. Try something different!

CHAPTER 4

The First Encounter: What Men Need To Do

"I just knew I had to meet her; it was pure impulse. I thought at this point, what have I got to lose?"

Bob

Many men embarking on first encounters frequently need a lot more help than women do. They may have been making social blunders with females since their high school years and don't know how to stop the pattern. Women, many men think, are more adaptable and intuitive and, from an earlier age, are more comfortable in new social situations.

To begin with, men who want to successfully play the midlife dating game should have an awareness of what women are seeking. As you will recall, the women in our survey ranked the following qualities they look for in a man: romantic and sexual (36 percent), educated and intelligent (28 percent), financially secure (19 percent), sense of humor (8 percent), spiritually aware (6 percent) and loyal and considerate (tied at 3 percent).

Like men, women have also evolved since high school or college. Then many women had one important goal—to get married. Now, in midlife, many women are looking for a significant relationship, which may or may not include marriage. A new relationship no longer hinges on the qualities women looked for when they were young, which frequently included the need for an athletic, handsome and popular man. Physical attractiveness came out far down on the list of primary qualities women in midlife perceive as important. Intelligence (which means a need for men to communicate) and romance (which includes the need for men to be sexually attentive) are now the top two qualities desired by more than 60 percent of women according to our survey.

How to Begin? Just Do It!

Men need to be fairly aggressive about approaching and meeting potential romantic partners. Men might want to approach the task of meeting women as though they are sales representatives making business calls—be positive, ask for the order and don't worry about rejection—just move on if she says no. Successful business executives remain positive about their chances for success no matter what the odds and always assume they will prevail in the end. Approaching and talking to women in a friendly and confident manner is no different. Try it and you'll be delighted when you see how well it works. Business rules also apply if you succeed in getting her telephone number. Call the next day, don't wait three or four days. Undue waiting makes you seem insecure or makes it look like you're playing youthful games and there is no need for such behavior at this stage of your life.

Some tips on your initial phone call: If she isn't there and you get an answering machine, just leave a message that you called and would like her to call you back. If she doesn't call back, there are three possible reasons and they are all indications that you should just forget it. First, no call back means she is inconsiderate or, second, she is just not interested. In either case, it's not worth your time to follow up. The third possibility is she didn't get your message, but be honest with yourself—that's doubtful. However, if you just have to try to meet this woman, call a second time, but don't get your hopes up. If she reciprocated your interest, she would have called you.

A man in our study, Bob, a forty-eight-year-old manager of a brokerage firm, had been recently transferred to Los Angeles. His first week there he went to a lively restaurant for lunch and had strong eye contact with a beautiful woman. On impulse, he went up to her, introduced himself, gave her his card and asked her to call him. She did so, although both later confessed to each other they had never done anything like this before. A year later, they are together and the chemistry is as strong as ever. Bob tells us, "At that moment, I just knew I had to try to meet her." The key element in Bob's new thought process: "What have I got to lose?"

Sam a forty-seven-year-old divorced man told us about one of his first dates. He was in a department store in Chicago selecting a necktie and impulsively asked a very attractive woman, Caroline, who was standing next to him which tie he should buy. In the next few minutes of conversation, he fell head over heels in love with her. Sam invited Caroline to lunch, then on a visit to a museum and, finally, to dinner—all in the same day! They closed the restaurant. She told him she loved his laugh, sense of humor, playfulness and the fact that he cancelled his afternoon and evening plans to be with her. They are still dating twelve months later and Sam has told his friends that he will soon propose. So you see, spontaneity works!

The women in our study remarked that their first-date wish list includes: a man who is interesting, passionate about life, radiates energy, has a passion for his work, projects a high degree of self- esteem, has solid values and has a healthy look. Our female respondents also stated that first impressions are very important. Therefore as we have said before, it is critical for men on a first date to understand they only get *one* chance to make that all important first impression. Said one woman, "I want a man with a young attitude who feels like life still has a lot more to offer." Gene, a fifty-eight-year-old man in our study, frequently gets told, "You look as if you have a healthy lifestyle and a happy face," which he takes as a great compliment—it helps him get dates.

Dress for Success

Appearance is crucial for men on a first date. Presumably, mature men now have significantly more knowledge, taste and judgment about how to dress than when they were in their twenties and thirties. They may also have the ability to afford a good quality wardrobe; however, being well groomed is within reach of everyone, regardless of economic status.

What should a man wear for a first encounter? Wearing a suit is a good idea if your date is in the evening or is for lunch during the week. You can't go wrong wearing a suit—it makes you look businesslike and professional. If suits are not your favorite, then be sure to wear something that gives the woman the sense that you have style and class, such as a leather jacket or sport coat, a white shirt (white shirts are a good choice because they look fresh and smart) and either tailored slacks or a good quality pair of jeans. Jeans with a sport coat and the clean lines of a white shirt can give you a very stylish look.

Shoes are critical, since it appears that a large percentage of the female population has a "thing" about shoes. Believe it or not, many women told us, shoes are frequently the first thing they notice about a man's appearance. This means you need to pay attention to your shoes. They most definitely need to be shined and, if expensive shoes are not in your budget, at least make sure they are not hiking boots or worse—sneakers. A seemingly little thing that women frequently notice: shoes and belts should be the same color and when in doubt dark is better than a light color when it comes to shoes.

Tom, a man in his early fifties who should have known better, recently walked through the San Francisco Tennis Club in old wrinkled jeans, shoes that looked like he had been wearing them for years without shining them and a faded shirt. When asked where he was going that evening, his response was, "I have a new date." Mason couldn't help himself and blurted out "What is she, a cleaning lady you want to bond with?" Tom, fortunately, had the strength of character to not take an attack on his attire personally, but he expressed puzzlement and was somewhat amazed that it would make a difference, since he viewed himself as a reasonably good-looking, smart and successful businessman (which he was). To no one's surprise, let it be reported here, there was no second date.

Take Charge!

Now that you have made a date, assume the initiative and take charge of the plans. If your first date is for dinner, select a restaurant and tell her your choice. The exception here would be if you are not familiar with restaurants in her area, in which case it is perfectly appropriate to ask her if she has a recommendation for a good place to eat. Choosing the venue also means you have an option about what you wear and the woman will have to dress accordingly. This has two advantages for you: First, it gives you a chance to look your best and second, it lets you see what kind of attire the woman will choose. A good reason to choose a restaurant or activity that requires wearing a suit or sport jacket is because a first date is somewhat like a job interview. You are selling the woman on your good qualities, and it would therefore seem logical to dress up rather than dress down. Many women respondents commented they liked this approach since it gave them a sense of the man's taste.

One caution does exist in the restaurant selection process. Many women in our survey said they appreciate being presented with alternatives. This means selecting two restaurants and giving the woman the chance to choose one of her liking. While many men might consider this unnecessary or a sign of high maintenance, women said they appreciated the courtesy of being given an option. Telling a woman you have two restaurants you are considering and asking her if she has a preference is certainly a reasonable alternative and will not make you seem indecisive; however, the initiator of the invitation, whether the man or the woman, should generally make the final choice.

Going to a play or a movie on a first date is generally a poor idea, since there is little opportunity for conversation. You can't learn much about a woman sitting in a dark room and not speaking. But if you do select this activity, try to end the evening with coffee or drinks so you can at least begin the process of getting to know one another.

If you don't like the dress up approach and you want to do something sporty or more casual, that will certainly work also. Just don't show up wearing something that will make her think you are a candidate for a homeless shelter.

In the final analysis, however, the type of activity doesn't really matter. Dinner, lunch, drinks or coffee, whatever you feel comfortable with as a first meeting, is what you should plan. Keep in mind, though, that it is highly risky to suggest an all day outing or some other lengthy event when you have not already spent time with your date, regardless of any bond or closeness you may have felt on the telephone or when you initially met her.

Compliments and Manners Are Appreciated

During the date, compliment her on her outfit, hairdo or her intelligence. Do not say things like, "You have a great body" or "You must go to the gym a lot." These comments are interpreted by women as sexual innuendos and are not considered flattering. Besides, most women want to be appreciated for who they are inside, not what they look like. You are already aware, of course, that most women do not respond positively to a foul mouth or bad language.

It is critical that you use the best manners you are capable of: open doors, walk on the outside of the sidewalk, help her on and off with her coat and pull out her chair in a restaurant to assist her in being seated. In short, do the little things you may have forgotten during your many years of marriage. Women are very attracted to men who behave like gentlemen and will give you a big mental plus for acting like one. Possibly, it would be worthwhile to read a book on etiquette to enhance your skills in that area.

There are some poor eating and drinking habits men have acquired that make very bad first impressions. Many women in our survey described first dates with men whose table manners were worse than those of their children. One woman told us of a first date who put an entire piece of bread into his mouth and then began smacking his lips. Another woman described her first date with a man who picked up the skin of a piece of fish he was eating (with his hands) and sucked on it. And yet another told us of her date endlessly gnawing on his lamb chop bones. You may think these situations are aberrations, but they seem to happen often enough that some men may need some guidance.

Gordon, a wealthy and well-known Philadelphia entrepreneur, recently had a blind date with Phoebe. She thought he was exactly what she had been seeking. But he drank five glasses of Chardonnay within two hours and then, while beginning to slur his words, described the restraining orders he had against his former wife. Needless to say, despite his many fine credentials, Phoebe decided he had far too many problems to deal with, including possible alcohol dependency. A key point—just because a man has been very successful in business does not mean he has had a lot of success in dealing with women or with relationships.

Be a Good Listener and Don't Brag

During the course of the date ask her opinion about a variety of topics, such as her job, her hobbies, what she likes to read, and show interest in her responses. Make her feel she is someone whose opinion you respect. If a woman feels genuine interest on your part, she will not only become more open with you, but she will be much more receptive to you as an individual.

A major error some men make is talking too much about themselves and how successful they are or how difficult their jobs are, rather than asking and listening to the woman's point of view. Certainly women are attracted to successful men, but going overboard with a long dissertation about your discovery of the cure for the world's monetary problems or how you leveraged your condo in Aspen into a real estate empire is not the way to impress her. Women can perceive confidence and sense success; you don't need to tell them. And nothing is more boring than a man who feels he is always right and insists on having the last word on any and every topic.

Bill was an interesting man who found Janet on the Internet. He was a vice president of a major technology company and had made several million dollars through stock options. She was very attracted to the fact that he was smart and successful, but he grossly overplayed his hand. After three months of dating at least three times a week, Janet didn't appreciate the fact that every conversation they had when they were around her friends eventually involved Bill's bragging about the number of new cars he owned, his new multimillion dollar house, the travel plans they had coming up or the five new three thousand dollar suits he had just purchased.

Janet had to make the drop decision even though the very qualities he bragged about were ones she liked. He was too much of a broken record about his wealth and success and that made him sound insecure to her and very shallow to her friends. Additionally, she had come to notice he didn't seem to have any friends of his own, either male or female, which is a warning sign women should note.

Also, when you are on the first date, don't talk about sports excessively or use sports analogies to describe your activities. There are women who are interested in sports, but if you don't know whether or not this is true of your date, hold the sports lingo for another time. Don't shoot yourself in the foot by using sports jargon or launching into an intense discussion of your favorite team.

Keep It Light

It is important that you make every attempt to keep the conversation fun and flirtatious, using humor and quips or light-hearted comments. Humor was very high on the desirable list of every woman surveyed. If you demonstrate that you possess such a quality, your stock goes up greatly. Don't have discussions about your terrible bad luck in your job or your marriage and please, do not discuss how you cheated on your wife or last girlfriend.

If the conversation turns more serious and personal, just go with it. There is nothing wrong with that kind of discussion if you both are seriously bonding and each of you feels comfortable going in that direction. One of the great things about getting older is that we can discuss personal subjects much more readily without fear of reproach from others; everyone has had ups and downs by this time in their lives. However don't sound bitter or negative when you talk about past life issues. Men need to be able to say something to the effect of, "I had this problem or this event happened, but I have moved on and I am looking forward to the next phase of my life."

William was a man with a substantial dating career who frequently found women saying to him, "I've never been this open with a man in my life on a first date." He finally concluded that women opened up to him because he was so frank and candid about his own life experiences. Women were so taken with his openness they simply found themselves reciprocating.

However, don't head in the direction of a total discussion of your inner feelings without some indication it will be reciprocated or is welcome.

One question men should probably avoid asking is their date's age. Many women are sensitive about this subject, often to the extreme that they won't tell anyone, even their best friend! Other questions to avoid are asking her what she wants in life and if she is looking for a relationship. Of course she is—just as you are. You are both there, aren't you? The "Do you want a relationship?" question is a rookie error made by many men and often may cause a woman to look upon you as a needy soul who is not worthy of a second date. You also should think about the ramifications of the answer to that question. What if she says she doesn't want a relationship; she just wants to date and have fun? Do you drop her because of one spontaneous comment?

Don't let your questions sound like you are conducting an interrogation; this is not conducive to a relaxed "getting-to-know-you" atmosphere. It can easily create an overall sense of tension and pressure, which is the last thing you want on any date.

Samantha, a fifty-four-year-old schoolteacher from the Portland area recently had a first date with Roger, a CEO of a large chemical company. During dinner, Roger, in a very clinical tone, asked her about every detail of her divorce, durations and particulars of recent relationships, and whether or not she had ever been in therapy and, if so, which kind.

There were so many questions that Samantha barely got to take a bite of her meal. Plus, the questions were far too intrusive and not necessarily the kind she wanted to answer on the first date, particularly a date in which there was no instant initial chemistry on her part. When they had finished dinner, Roger asked her if she wanted an after dinner drink. Samantha, to use our backgammon analogy, dropped out of the game and opted for an early evening.

Pay Attention. Don't Be a Bore!

If you have obvious (and we mean obvious) mutual chemistry on your first date, then you may want to consider playfulness that includes casual physical touching, but don't make major aggressive moves or make a suggestion that a sexual conclusion to the date may be in order. Just play out the date and let things unfold. Most women enjoy flirting, hand holding and a casual arm around their shoulders. Men who are good flirters are perceived as good lovers. At the end of the evening and when you are alone, you may make an overt but not overly aggressive physical move. But do this only if you feel it will be accepted, otherwise you will seem like a bumbling amateur to her.

The woman will basically decide (in fact, she has already decided one way or the other—you just don't yet know her decision) how fast the physical relationship will proceed that night. Most women reported they know within the first ten minutes of meeting a new man if there is any physical chemistry present.

Forcing affection on a woman at the end of the first date is another rookie error and you deserve rejection if you try it without some indication your date will be receptive. In fact, just saying "Goodnight" will be perceived as a very classy and gentlemanly act by virtually every woman. One of the comments consistently made by women in our survey was that women appreciated the fact that most men in midlife are less aggressive about pushing sex during the early dates than they may have been in their youths.

This advice, of course, excludes the instant physical and mental chemistry date, in which all personal details of your lives are discussed and which may even lead to spending the night (an acceptable outcome if both parties agree).

Don't Be Argumentative

It is possible you may find yourself in a discussion that escalates to something that borders on argumentative. If you find yourself headed in this direction, you need to stop for a few seconds and decide if this is really where you want to go. If you have future desires for this woman, you should de-escalate any passionate discussions that could be perceived by your date as seriously challenging her intellect or as being unduly argumentative.

While many men can have a very heated argument with another male friend and just walk away and forget it, some women do not behave this way. They may remember the incident for a long time and even hold permanent grudges toward the men who seriously argue with them or put them down in a manner perceived to be clinical. Every man should know that being argumentative with a woman is not the way to win her heart or endear himself to her.

However, if you decide the date is not one that is going to result in a follow-up, then it may be the only thing you have to keep the evening interesting. If so, then use the disagreement as a mental exercise and consider it a form of entertainment. At least that may make the evening lively. Just remember, this woman will probably consider you an ass for the rest of her natural life. She will definitely tell her friends, and since you don't want a bad reputation, behaving like a gentleman during the date is your best option.

Read My Mind? I Don't Think So!

Mark had a first dinner date with Susan, to whom he was introduced by mutual friends. Mark was a very private person and was not known for his communication skills, and had had a dreadful day at the office. He felt Susan should be able to sense this and he was very disappointed that she didn't try to find out what was bothering him. He expected her to read his mind and when she didn't he grew more sullen as the dinner progressed. He did not call Susan again and while she knew there was a problem, she had been unable to put her finger on what it was.

If you are like Mark, you will need to learn to be more open about your feelings. Women often equate talking with real communication and they cannot read your mind. Tell them what you are thinking, and you will be amazed at the positive responses you get. Just don't make the discussion so depressing they want to leave as soon as dinner is over.

Negativity Is a Killer

A key point worth emphasizing: Avoid any negative comments about your ex-wife or former girlfriends during the date. This sort of talk makes it seem like you have an axe to grind, or worse, it makes you sound bitter. If you and your date have any conversations about exes, make sure to keep it positive during this initial encounter. Negativism and cynicism are a turn-off no matter what the topic, but when in reference to an ex it can project a particularly terrible image.

Speaking negatively about former spouses seems to happen more often with men than with women, possibly because of the financial losses men may have suffered in their divorce settlements. It is a pitfall men should avoid at all costs. Most people believe compensation is justified for wives who have spent a lifetime bringing up children and running a home; men will do themselves no favors by harping on this issue.

Never Kiss and Tell. It's An Unforgivable Amateur Error.

If you are successful in having sex with your date, regardless of when it occurs, on the first date or much later, do not ever, ever have a discussion with others about it. Do not talk about your date to others, men or women friends, in any way that indicates there was sex. Other than showing a lack of propriety, there are practical considerations.

If you mention her name, or your friend knows who she is, it is very likely that he, in turn, will tell someone else, either his girlfriend or his wife or even some other man. You don't need this kind of information spread around. You are not twenty anymore and no one needs to know what you do with your women friends. If you kiss and tell, there is a reasonable probability the she or one of her friends will hear that you're spreading the story and then you will have real trouble.

Call Sooner, Not Later

After the first date, if you find you are greatly attracted to this woman and you sincerely want to get to know her better, it is appropriate to send her a card or call to tell her you had a great time. Do not overwhelm her with cards, flowers, E-mails, letters or other gifts in an attempt to make an impression on her. Many women will react negatively to this behavior and may see this as the conduct of a desperate and needy man. She will not only fail to respond in the manner in which you desire, but she most likely will not want to have a second date with you.

Be a Gentleman and Be Respectful

To be successful in dating, you will not go wrong adhering to the key principals we have discussed is this chapter.
— Be spontaneous or be formal, but follow through when you see a woman you think you would like to get to know better.
— Dress nicely and be well-groomed.
— Be complimentary to your date and show good manners.
— Be a good listener and put a lid on the bragging.
— Keep the conversation light—at least at first. Don't interrogate your date; follow her lead as to how intense the conversation gets.
— Show interest in what she says and don't be argumentative.
— A gentleman is always discreet.

Once men understand these basic rules, their chance at a second act can begin.

Quiz – Chapter 4

For men only: Do you understand what you need to do on a first encounter? This quick quiz will help you evaluate your knowledge of first dates. Please rate yourself:

10 points for a "yes"; 5 points for an "undecided"; 0 points for a "no"

Ranking	Question
_____	1. I would approach an attractive woman I don't know.
_____	2. Once I have met a woman I want to see again, I have enough self-confidence to contact her.
_____	3. I understand the importance of "first impressions" on a date and I dress my best and carefully watch my manners.
_____	4. On a first encounter, I try to draw my date out and limit talk about myself.
_____	5. I do not talk negatively about my ex-wife or girlfriends.
_____	6. I do not "gossip" and discuss past dates with my current date.
_____	7. If my date indicates she in not interested in sexual overtures, I accept this and behave like a gentleman.

Scoring

70 – 60 - You are a man who clearly understands what you need to do on a first date to attract a woman.

50-40 - You are getting there. Notice how your friends who are successful with women attract them.

20 – 0 - You need to become more aggressive in your social life. The last we heard, sitting home alone isn't all that great!

CHAPTER 5

The First Encounter:
What Women Need To Do

"It's a myth that men like dumb women."
Arthur

If a woman wants to attract a man, she needs to know what he is seeking. According to our survey, men are looking for: compatibility and common interests (34 percent), physical attractiveness (22 percent), intelligence (17 percent), romantic and sexual (13 percent), fun and with a lot of common interests (9 percent), and financially sound (5 percent). Once you understand this, you will be better equipped to capture his attention.

The First Date: How It Works

As in all events, a first date has a clear beginning, middle and an end. Let's start with the basics of a first encounter. How do women handle the logistics of their first date? If you haven't dated in a number of years, you may find everything has changed. If you have previously met the man or are aware of his background from a mutual friend, then the simple, traditional answer is to have him come and pick you up at your home. But this is another era and things are not as simple as they once were—there are new complexities to consider.

Let's say you live some distance away from your date, over twenty miles or more. Then it might be more appropriate to agree to meet halfway at some agreeable location. "Why?" you ask. "I have never driven to meet a man." Meeting halfway is not a sign of weakness or bending to a man's will, nor is it an inconsiderate request by a boorish man. It is just simple courtesy to save him an excessive time commitment. You have to consider that one half-hour to pick you up, another half-hour to get to the restaurant, then a half-hour to take you home and then a final half-hour to drive himself home is two hours of driving! While you may not consider that to be excessive, it is a lot to ask of a man who does not really know you.

Another good reason to meet a man somewhere, particularly on a first date, rather than have him pick you up is that this way you have a means of escape if the date becomes tedious or he is obnoxious.

If this man is someone you don't know very well or someone you don't know at all, you surely will want to meet him at a neutral location before you decide to invite him to your home. This is especially true if it is a blind date about whom you have virtually no information. This is a safety issue, but if he is truly not interesting, or worse, the date from hell, you are definitely in a better position to cut the date short and leave if you have your own transportation as a means of escape.

Leigh, a woman in our study, told us about her first date. He came to her home to pick her up for dinner and she made the mistake (in retrospect) of asking him if he wanted a quick drink before leaving. She opened a bottle of chardonnay and he proceeded to have one, then two, and then three drinks. When he excused himself to go to the rest room, he was very unsteady on his feet. Needless to say, when he returned, she excused herself from going out with him for the evening. Leigh was lucky, because she was able to extricate herself early from what would have been a bad evening. This is clearly a good example of why one should drive one's own car or arrange to meet at a neutral location.

Where to Go

There is always the issue of what *kind* of a date to have. The most logical and simple options are dinner, lunch, a drink after work or coffee. Lunch can be a good option if you are both working in the same city or general area. Our survey participants advise that from both a time and expense point of view, dinners on the first meeting generally are not in anyone's best interest. An entire evening may be more time than you want for a first date. An exception may be made if the man is someone you already know you want to spend time with, or has a very high recommendation from a close friend. As an incidental note, if the man asked you out, he should pay for the first date. Splitting the check is reasonable, but only if the woman asked out the man.

First Impressions

So now you have a date and you know where to meet—you are at the critical juncture. An old truth, but it's more important than ever: *You don't get a second chance to make a first impression.* Just as we counseled men in the previous chapter, your hair, grooming and clothing are important. You need to pay special attention to how you look. Remember, "chemistry" to most men means they find a woman visually appealing. If, in fact, you are wearing a baggy dress and have your hair tied up in a way that makes you look like you have been cleaning the house, the chemistry opportunity will not be optimal.

Overdoing makeup can be a big deal to some men. Don't try to disguise yourself. Many women will often resort to additional makeup in an attempt to hide the aging process. This is a trap you should try to avoid. You will be amazed at how much more receptive men are to a natural look.

If you are invited to an evening that includes dinner or cocktails, wear a business like outfit that shows you as a sophisticated woman or, if this is not your style, then wear a casual but conservative dress. Do not wear a low-cut or sexy outfit or dress—your goal on the first date is to blend in, not create a statement about your terrific body.

Ed, a forty-seven-year-old never-married bachelor, was at a party and found himself in a discussion with two very elegant and conservatively dressed women. They teasingly asked him if they should have worn low cut, sexy dresses since a lot of the men seemed to be talking to women who did. His answer was, "The men are talking to those women because they are sexually on the prowl and they think they have a chance for a quick score. They are not thinking 'this is the woman I want my mother to meet or that I want to take to the next office party.' They are simply resorting to their base sexual instincts."

It's a fact that many men spend a greater part of their day looking at women—even when they are committed to a monogamous relationship or married. This is just a part of what most men do. It's an ingrained trait. So even though they may not say anything, they are very aware of how you look. Keep in mind the event and the place you are to meet; it is important that your clothing fit the occasion. If the man doesn't tell you the nature of the event, it is okay to ask him what sort of attire you should wear.

What to Say, What Not to Say

You are finally on the date! What do you say, or not say, as the case may be? First, you need to be open and honest. Keep in mind, most men are not the suave conversationalists you saw in those old Cary Grant movies. Men sometimes ask very personal and direct questions, not because they are being insensitive, but because they may not know what else to talk about. Often men lack the small "chit-chat" conversational skills that many women have developed over the years. You may have to take the lead in generating a conversation. Also many men, because of their business backgrounds, may tend to be bottom line oriented—they want the facts as soon as possible. This means you will have to decide how open and deep you want to be with your date. It also means you shouldn't judge a man too harshly just because he appears very aggressive in wanting to know facts about your life—unless, of course, he gets too personal.

Don't slip and make the rookie error comment one woman recently made: "My good friend Alice is really lucky. She just got married." It sounded like her friend was saved from the horrible fate of being single. Don't project the feeling that being single is a horrible fate or you will risk coming across as a helpless, needy soul and that is definitely not your goal! Don't affect an aura of mystery or set yourself up as an insurmountable challenge. Most mature men don't need new challenges in their life. They have enough of them to deal with in their jobs and certainly want to avoid any of those types of problems that may have existed in their former relationships. Men generally don't want to play games and try to solve the mystery of who you are; they just want to know certain facts about your life. Remember, men tend to be bottom-line oriented—it means they want reasonable answers to reasonable questions.

Disclosing Personal Information

As with many areas of dating you need to use your intuition and go with your feelings in disclosing personal information. Some people do very well with complete candor on the first or second date. Others feel they need to maintain a degree of privacy. You will need to judge what works best on a case-by-case basis. Generally speaking, however, men and women who are older tend to be more open and forthcoming in discussing their past and current lives. Indeed, many are eager to have these conversations. As the date unfolds, you will know if there is a basic chemistry between the two of you, so opening up and telling a man personal details about yourself and your life may just seem a very natural thing to do. Follow your instincts—if it seems natural and appropriate, say it!

If a woman asks him during a first date, Mason will disclose anything about his personal life. His attitude is, if she doesn't like the answer, she can make it the first and last date. An overwhelming percentage of his dates respond positively to this kind of honesty and openness and frequently reciprocate. So getting highly personal in your revelations is certainly an okay thing to do. Drawing someone out has one other great benefit. If you hear something that is simply too outrageous for your sensibilities, you may save yourself a lot of time by not scheduling a second date!

Nancy thinks you should not ask a man anything you are not willing to answer yourself. Several times, however, she has asked a casual question only to be taken aback when her date answered more openly and in greater detail than she expected. She, like many women, does not like to make her life an open book on the first few dates and does not respond well to men who do so. If you are not willing to be open with your date, you cannot expect him to be open. In this scenario, you may defeat the very purpose of the date—to get to know someone!

It is also important not to have the conversation sound like you are conducting an interrogation or a job interview. This will come across as too clinical. Just ask the kinds of things that seem natural, which could include something like, "How long since you've been in a relationship? How did your last relationship end?" If your date doesn't want to answer he may well say, "I don't want to talk about it" and that, in turn, might be an early indication of someone who is still in emotional pain or is just not able to talk about his feelings. In either case, it is an early sign that should be duly noted and taken into consideration as you progress through the date.

Sometimes, you can be in for a huge surprise, like Maggie, who had an unforgettable first date. She met Clarke at a church dance and had a wonderful time twirling around the floor with him for most of the evening. He invited her to a dance in a nearby city the following Saturday night and she accepted. That night, much to her surprise, in a short period of time Clarke got very drunk. There had been no alcohol at the church dance, so she had no way to anticipate this problem.

Clarke proceeded to get very loud and belligerent and Maggie realized she would not be safe driving home in his car. She had a hard time getting a cab, then realized she had not brought money with her—a mistake she will never make again. When she got to her house (a thirty-minute taxi ride), she had to write an sixty-five dollar check, begging the driver to accept it. Clarke never called to apologize and when he saw her at the next church dance, he acted as if nothing had happened. The moral is never travel too far from you own area too early in the dating cycle, but if you do—carry cash.

Remember Your Manners

For both men and women, the protocol of going on a date means they expect a certain type of behavior, a certain level of courtesy and manners. If a man suggests a specific restaurant, you should not say "I don't like that restaurant, let's not go there" or worse, once you get there, complain about the location of your table, the food, the wine or the service. It makes you sound like a whiner and that's something that turns off most men. The exception to this is if you have a genuine objection to that particular restaurant, such as a strong aversion to the type of food or a history with a former relationship that makes it painful to go there. In those situations, simply state the reason why you would prefer another dinner choice.

A friend of Mason's had two dinner dates last year with a woman who sent the food back both times, because she "didn't like the way it was prepared." This kind of behavior is likely to motivate any man to question why he is there in the first place. And Nancy has a friend who regularly takes a sip of her wine and sends the bottle back as "not quite up to standards." The friend wonders why she is not invited out a second time.

Being overly sensitive and making accusatory comments when a man talks to another woman friend while you are on a date (assuming it is not a lengthy conversation and you are not ignored) is also a rookie error and makes you seem very insecure. This goes beyond the first date and is a rule women should adhere to at all times.

Being Aware

Good conversationalists are always popular and one can learn this art by keeping up with the news, social trends and popular culture. Eileen, one of our survey participants, often reads the *Wall Street Journal* before a date and makes a short list of four current topics. During a lull in the conversation, she brings them up and asks her date's opinion. He is not only impressed that she is interested in the latest news, but flattered that she wants to know his thoughts. From your perspective, this will give you an idea about his competence in current event knowledge. Please be aware that this can be dangerous if you sound rehearsed or superficial or don't have sufficient background to respond to any comeback questions.

Art, one of the men in our study, says he speaks for the majority of men when he says, "It is a myth that men like dumb women." The mature man considers a woman he dates over a period of time to be somewhat of a reflection of himself and most men do not want a woman who has all of his friends or his children muttering about what a bad choice he made. Men want someone who is both articulate and has the ability to converse with a variety of people about a wide number of subjects.

Now, if you are a really smart woman, flaunt it, don't hide it. Most mature men are highly attracted to this quality in women. Don't downplay advanced degrees or impressive job titles. Just one caveat: do not behave in a superior or argumentative manner and don't insist you are right on every point. Most men will flee in an instant if a woman appears to challenge, disagree or argue about insignificant points in almost every discussion. Just as women do not appreciate an argumentative man, men have an equally critical view of the argumentative woman. Don't confuse being assertive with being argumentative—they are very different.

The Story of Veronica Franco

The female counterpart to Casanova is a woman named Veronica Franco, a courtesan who lived in Venice from 1546 to 1591. Veronica was so well known that a movie was made about her life called *Dangerous Beauty*. She became allied with some of the most powerful men of the period, who associated with her not just for her sexual prowess, but also for her company. Her literary skills, wit, conversational ability and poetry made her one of the most famous and sought-after courtesans of that time period. All women, at any age, can develop charm and women who project an engaging, pleasant personality will always be in demand.

This is certainly not a call for women to become courtesans, but it is illustrative of how knowledgeable women can become desirable. Veronica Franco, incidentally, was not a great beauty; she was an average-looking woman who merely used her mind and great charm to her utmost advantage.

Sex: Now or Later?

Often, the subject of sex arises on the first date. As you well know, things have changed substantially since you were in your twenties. Before the sexual revolution of the sixties many women stayed celibate until marriage for religious or cultural reasons or because this is what they thought men wanted. In those years men sometimes married a woman because he thought it was the only way he could have sex with her.

Stories abound about men who have said, "When I was in my twenties, I wanted to have regular sex and I also had a career to start which was taking a lot of time. So I found what seemed like a nice girl who would make a good mother and just got married to solve the problem." So why do you think there is a very large percentage of divorces today? We all grew up!

Men were not created in a vacuum and they remember how they reacted to the withholding of sex by women when they were young. More likely than not, they are going to be unwilling to accept this position today. Even though you may be withholding sex for an entirely different reason today, some men may simply give up in favor of a more sexually approachable woman. Most men, not all, but most, are no longer susceptible to coy behavior on the part of a potential romantic partner. Your best strategy on a first date is to try to stay away from sex as a subject; you probably have nothing to gain. Again, all of this advice goes out the window if you find yourself in one of those instant chemistry situations when everything is discussed openly.

Annie told us about her relationships. "I had a failed marriage, then a failed relationship. Finally I thought I had found the right person—I had instant chemistry with him. I thought if we had sex on the second date, it would be okay. I thought he really cared for me, but he never called back." Although sex at an early stage will not make or break a relationship, it also isn't the reason a man does not call back. Annie lost the guy, but having sex on the second date was not the reason. He just wasn't interested in her.

The decision about when to have sex is an individual issue, but don't think that having sex at an early stage in the relationship was the reason why you were rejected. It simply does not work that way for most men. You can take the advice of some psychologists today and withhold sex until you believe he is fully committed to you, but understand that many men may just decide to find another woman. Obviously, you should not do anything with which you are not comfortable.

So now you are nearing the end of the first date. If he pressures you to have sex and you are not interested, you may just want to terminate the date for cause. No man who is truly interested in you will pressure you to do anything you do not want to do. Men who resort to pressure are either insecure or simply have no respect for you—they want their desires fulfilled regardless of what you think. So do not be insecure about showing such a man the door. He will not be back anyway.

When Sex Seems Okay

All of this advice goes out the window if you find yourself in one of those instant chemistry situations when everything is discussed openly and you decide to have sex immediately. There are hundreds of examples of men who married women with whom they had sex on the first date. Sex on the first date is not—repeat not—a negative to many men. They just see it as a fantastic end to an evening and will probably look forward to the next date. If nothing happens later, it wasn't meant to be, but it is not because you had sex. If it *is* the reason, then you just had sex with a very insecure man, probably with tons of low self-esteem. Don't dwell on it, just move on.

Be Cautious, But Not Paranoid

If you decide to have sex on the first date or anytime early in the relationship, for that matter, it is highly advisable to ask the man to use a condom. Although men traditionally seem to worry less about sexually transmitted diseases than women, they may *want* to use a condom. You never really know about the complete sexual history of someone you just met. Those who have strong feelings may ask their potential partner to take a full battery of medical tests before any physical intimacy.

A Potential Dilemma for Women

Now you've made the decision that you *do* want to have sex with this man, but you *do* want to use a condom. You may need to supply them yourself. If you are at his house it is more than likely not a problem since he should have them, but if you are at your house, it's a different situation. This may shock you, but most men are not walking around with condoms in their wallets with the wild optimism that sex is just around the corner, like they did when they were teenagers or in college. So if you are a woman and sex at your house is a possibility, you will need to head to the local drugstore (or buy them on the Internet if you are too embarrassed) to get your supply.

There are many wonderful jokes about women buying condoms. Nancy's favorite is about the nun who wasn't allowed to smoke in the convent, but who snuck her cigarettes onto the patio. To keep her cigarettes dry when it rained, another nun showed her how to put a condom over them. The nun decided to purchase some of her own and when the druggist asked her what size, she replied, "I don't know, just so long as it fits my Camel."

There is one male attitude about which women should be aware. There is a percentage of men who will refuse to wear a condom under any circumstance. Their logic is, "It doesn't feel right" or something to that effect. Mason's feeling is that women should react by essentially responding, "Goodbye" or "You're out of here." A man who refuses to wear a condom is essentially saying, "I have no respect for you as a woman, my desires take precedence over your concerns about disease." In effect he is saying "Trust me."

Trust you? I don't think so.

Follow Up

Now that your first date is over and it is the day after—should you call him? The answer is sure, if you are so inclined and if you want to express the fact you had a good time. It's mannerly and most men will appreciate hearing from you. Nancy sometimes sends a short E-mail to thank her date for a nice evening. She often sends it just after her date leaves, so he will receive it when he gets home. The key, however, is not to overdo contacting him until you have had enough dates to feel comfortable that it is a two-way relationship.

However, there may be situations in which the man is very shy or insecure around women or he may even feel intimidated for some reason. If you feel this may be the case and you enjoyed his company, it's fine to call him and ask him out for lunch, some other event you know about, or perhaps a home-cooked meal. He will probably be very happy you called.

If, however, you call him and you get lines like, "I am really busy with work," or "I've been traveling a lot lately" or "I just have a lot of things on my mind right now," you will know that it is not to be. All of these remarks are just cover statements designed not to hurt your feelings and to cop out of the situation.

Another Quandary: Is He Sincere or a Manipulator?

A man's follow-up process can be confusing. Figuring out his motive can be complicated for a woman who's had the big rush put on her after the first date: cards, flowers and frequent calling. So here are the possibilities you should consider when a man sends a card or flowers after the first date.

First, he may be needy and feels he should try to do something to win you over. Second, he could be a Casanova-type or worse, an abusive or narcissistic man in disguise attempting to get you to think he is sincere and romantic. This is a standard ploy to get you to have sex sooner rather than later. And third, he *is* sincere and really just wants to send a message that he truly is interested and appreciates you.

Here is another instance in which the midlife dating game is different from your experiences in your younger days. While it is true that flowers or cards after the first date may be a part of a Casanova strategy, it is far less likely behavior for a man in his middle or later years. At this stage of a man's life, it is much more probable that this is meant as a truly romantic gesture and the man is sincerely interested. Mature men don't usually waste time playing a game or pursuing a hard to get strategy. Sending a card or flowers is one way they let a woman know they want to pursue a relationship.

Finally, if you are subjected to significant unwanted attention after a first date, even when it should be obvious you did *not* have a great time, you will need to be firm and friendly and reject the overtures. Simply say, "I am sorry, you are just not my type," or "I am too involved with work to go out again right now, but I hope we can be friends." If you feel he is an interesting man, you may want to suggest he go out with one of your friends as an alternative. Again, a self-assured man will consider it a compliment that, although he is not your type, you thought enough of him to introduce him to one of your friends.

Just as a warning, there are a few men out there who will not take "no" for an answer regardless of what you say. These men will continue to call or e-mail you even if you have told them repeatedly you are not interested. Fortunately these are relatively rare situations and it goes without saying that excessive attention of this nature is abnormal and men who display it are to be avoided.

Drop or Accept

Keep in mind that most men have a long history of rejection and they therefore have little ego involved when you say "no." They have spent the major portion of their lives being rejected by women, starting in high school when they began to date, up to the time they got married and now continuing when they are again single. Most men have been rejected by women far more than they have been accepted, so this is nothing new. Men do the asking, therefore they more often get rejected; it is just a statistical fact of life.

If a man calls and asks you out at a time you are busy, but you want to go out with him, give him a modern day answer. Suggest an alternative day, such as, "I can't go out Thursday, but I am free on Friday or next Tuesday." Men appreciate being given this sort of straightforward answer and encouragement.

There is another early dating scenario that frequently occurs and which requires women to make decisions. You are dating a man you would like to get to know better, but you have made it clear that you do not yet want to have sex with him. Then he asks you to go on a short weekend trip.

What do you do? Assuming you would like to go with him, your options are: not to go, go and take your chances you will not have to fend him off or have a discussion about sleeping arrangements in advance. The sensible answer clearly is to have an honest, heart-to-heart discussion prior to the trip.

Joan, a fifty-two-year-old woman in our study, decided to tell her suitor she would love to travel with him, but she needed a separate room. Since she was aware of the potential burden of the added expense, she told him that if he wanted to keep expenses down, she would also stay in the same room with him with a separate bed and a pledge from him that he would not expect sex. He agreed and they had a lovely weekend during which he remained a perfect gentleman. The weekend turned out to be the basis for a long and wonderful relationship. This worked well for Joan, however, the risk is that the man agrees to the conditions, but does not abide by them once you arrive at your destination. If you have any great worry about this turn of events and feel you don't totally trust the man to live up to his commitments then don't go. Of course, you may go and change your mind during the weekend and decide, "Now is the time" and have sex. In which case, you are both in a win-win situation.

Take Care of Me?

Many of the women in our survey stated they had a fear of finding a man who would need to be "taken care of." One woman aptly summarized the feelings of many when she told us about Mitch. She said, "Mitch lost his wife of nearly forty years and he seemed truly lost. I was one of the first women he dated. We soon got into a relationship and Mitch expected me to do a lot of the things his wife had done. I found myself taking his shirts to the cleaners, running errands, buying many of his groceries and cooking his dinners. I soon felt like a cross between a maid, a cleaning service and a cook. I realized I did not need that kind of relationship and I opted out. I continued to be Mitch's friend, and saw him finally evolve to become much more independent and understanding about what women want. But when I first met him, it was just too early."

Be an Internet Detective

There is something you can do before you have the first date with a new man: Look him up on the Internet. This is an information option that should not be ignored. Recently, Kay, an elegant woman in her mid-forties, met a charming man at a cocktail party and they exchanged cards. His card had the web site of his company listed. Out of curiosity she looked up the web site name (his card said he was the executive vice president of a commodities trading company) and found the site was no longer available—the company had been dissolved. One of the reasons to check the web site of the company is that his biography will undoubtedly be shown if he is a significant employee. To find out any specifics that may be available about him just enter his name on one of the Internet search engines, such as Google, Alltheweb or Yahoo.

That Pesky, Yet All Important First Date

The collective advice of the over 400 people in our survey and the more than 1,000 people we talked to validate that the first date is an important one: it sets the tone for the next stage of the relationship as well as lets the two people involved know if they even want to *have* a second date. So let's review some key points.

— Take special care with your appearance and dress.
— Have interesting things to talk about and keep the conversation flowing.
— Be open and honest.
— Don't appear needy.
— Captivate him with your charm.
— Be true to yourself regarding sex, but don't be coy or insincere.
— Ask him questions and listen carefully to his answers. Use the knowledge you gain to assess the compatibility of your date.

Most men and women in our study confided that after a normal first date, they could have gone either way on whether or not to have a second date. For most of us on a first date, the bells and whistles are just not that noticeable. If this is the case on your first date, it probably makes sense to go out again just to see if there is anything about the person that motivates you to continue. However, many of us have had at least one experience of "being struck by lightening" and know we have met a very special person. When this happens, and a soul mate enters our life, all the conventional words of wisdom go out the window, and a powerful connection and chemistry seem to take over. *There is nothing wrong with this feeling*—not at this stage of your life.

Quiz – Chapter 5

For women only: Do you understand what men are seeking? This knowledge will significantly improve your chances of a relationship. This quick quiz will help you evaluate whether or not you really know what men want. Please rate yourself:

10 points for a "yes"; 5 points for an "undecided"; 0 points for a "no"

Ranking	Question
_____	1. I am comfortable suggesting where to meet for a first date.
_____	2. I am astute enough to recognize that excessive attention after a first date is a warning signal.
_____	3. I am able to have an easy "give and take" conversation with most of my first dates.
_____	4. If a man asks me questions that are more personal than I want to answer, I can handle the situation.
_____	5. I know the key topics that I should stay away from on a first date.
_____	6. I could have a discussion with a man about going away for a weekend, explain I didn't want to have sex and be comfortable with the conversation.
_____	7. After a date, I am confident contacting my escort to thank him for a good time.

Scoring

70 – 60 - You are a very savvy woman with a good understanding of how to deal with men.

50 – 30 - You are not a good observer of the opposite sex. Be more perceptive!

20 – 0 - It would help to be more straightforward and open in your approach.

CHAPTER 6

Male and Female Posturing and Communication: The Good, the Bad and the Ugly

"I made an early decision not to waste time with what appeared to be a dead end relationship."

Doreen

How do males and females position themselves and communicate on a new date? Our research showed there is a distinct difference between the sexes. Since the first date sets the stage for the next one, positioning yourself in the most favorable light is crucial. The key, particularly for men, is not to dominate the discussion with braggadocio that makes you sound arrogant. When in doubt, be humble. No one appreciates a long dialogue about how wonderful you are on the first date—a fault that for some reason seems to belong almost exclusively to men.

One advantage of being in midlife or older is that mature men and woman can be very intuitive and can make pretty good initial judgments about other people. Trusting your first impression of someone on a first date may now be a capability you need to recognize you possess. It should be noted, however, that there is a countervailing theory promoted by many psychologists which says that you should not make snap judgments and you should not reject a follow-up date based on a negative or neutral first impression. Only you can figure out if that response is right for you. But regardless of whether this advice is right or wrong, it is still a fact that in the real world the response by the vast majority of people is to end the relationship with the first encounter if there is no initial chemistry.

Two Egregious Errors

A first date scenario: Barry, a fifty-nine-year-old divorced man, has asked a woman out and they are halfway through dinner. The woman, Jane, is smart, elegant and independent, with a consulting practice of her own. She is recently divorced after twenty-five years. Barry's initial reaction is one of high interest and he is already contemplating future dates and possibly a relationship.

The dinner conversation that evening ranges from Jane's consulting practice and the newly found independence she developed after her divorce. In short, Barry and Jane bond during this first encounter. They are both enthusiastic, interesting to each other and in a flirting mode. As they discover more and more similar interests, they mentally project other dates involving activities they both enjoy.

As frequently occurs, the conversation eventually gets around to relationships. Barry, at this point, is already thinking of a good spot to have a comfortable after dinner drink and discussion. Then comes a small, seemingly harmless statement from his date, "I really want to find a committed relationship; I really don't like being single."

Well, Barry thinks, *maybe it's a little soon for that kind of discussion, but that's okay, it's an honest statement, and that's what I eventually want too.* Then Jane delivers the coup de grace…"I really wouldn't consider a physical relationship with a man who wasn't totally committed to me and whom I didn't intend to marry." Kaboom! Barry's intake of food accelerated at an exponential rate. Dessert? "No, thanks." After dinner drink? "No, thanks." "Waiter, check please, I have an early tennis game." Barry has her in her driveway by nine-thirty that night. "Want to come in for a coffee?' she asks. "No thanks," says Barry, "I have an early morning."

But, not willing to leave well enough alone, Barry now decides to shoot himself in the foot by launching into a lecture as he walks her to the door. "Do you realize you are now fifty years old and you are probably going to date men who are older, maybe even in their sixties? These men are not necessarily in great shape and they certainly aren't going to have sex multiple times a week, in fact, their interest in sex is waning as we speak. 'You don't get older, you just get better,' is a myth. People that espouse that theory clearly had a boring and uneventful youth.

"There is absolutely nothing physically good about men getting old. A woman who is waiting for the ultimate man and ultimate situation may have a very long wait and she may never find him. Have you noticed some of your dates even now can't walk up a couple of hills without getting winded? So, what are you waiting for? Men aren't getting better—sex will soon be something you won't have to worry about at all." Barry, almost breathless himself after delivery this diatribe, finally stops talking. Jane, a horrified look on her face, sticks out her hand, shakes his and says, "Good night." They never see each other again.

Certainly some women (and some men also) truly want to wait for sex until marriage or at least a committed relationship and there is nothing wrong with that attitude if both parties are in agreement. The key here is to find a partner with similar thoughts. Whatever your values, there are many good men out there with similar principles. In the case of Barry and Jane, there were clearly different value systems in play.

The key question raised by this story, however, is why throw down the gauntlet, so to speak, and create what appears to be an ultimatum about anything on the first date?

Does this mean you shouldn't be honest about what you want or that you shouldn't talk about relationships? Absolutely not—honesty is crucial. But on a first or second date you need to have some sense of timing as to when you should share this more detailed information, which incidentally, in retrospect, you might not really mean. Many women and men not only change their minds, they really didn't mean what they said in the first place. Of course, Barry's diatribe was stupid. His speech sounded sophomoric and he insulted his date's intelligence.

First of all, Jane may not have totally meant what she said about remaining celibate until she and her partner were committed. It may have been her way of letting Barry know she was interested in a serious relationship and didn't like dating around. And even if she did mean it at the time, there is a probability she would change her mind if she fell in love, but Barry chose not to find out. The potential for a relationship was there, but both Barry and Jane shot it down.

A Rookie Error

The error Jane made was making statements that sounded non-negotiable. What Barry heard was, "I need to know your intentions now. I don't even know if I like you or not, but I want to know your motives." If you stop to think about what Jane said, it almost forced Barry to make a decision on the first date as to whether or not he wanted a serious relationship. Some men take such a statement to mean, "Don't date me unless you intend to have a monogamous relationship with me." Most women didn't do this when they were younger, why do it now? Is it because they think time is running out? This statement also puts a lot of pressure on the man, who may not respond well to pressure in the first place, to immediately start thinking in serious terms about his date. Remember, you have just met! Why not just have at least a couple of dates and then decide if you are interested in pursuing a relationship?

Women should not have discussions about wanting a meaningful and monogamous relationship before the man can even begin to get interested. While a serious and fulfilling relationship is certainly the goal of the vast majority of both sexes, it can often be overwhelming to many men to hear this before they even get through dinner. So it's fine to have the conversation, but be patient and wait until he gets to know you a little bit.

No Sex? Just Tell Him

There is another related sexual situation that is more often than not a woman's issue and involves the avoidance of sex. Since men rarely want to avoid sex, this circumstance seldom applies in reverse, although it certainly could. The situation arises when a woman begins dating a man she enjoys and wants to continue seeing, but with whom she does not wish to have sex. It may be that she absolutely knows she does not ever want to sleep with this particular man or it may be that she needs more time to decide if she wants to take this step.

The man, however, is thinking it is time to start considering sexual activity and will begin making suggestive comments or physical moves. So the question is, if you find yourself in this scenario, how should you deal with it? The simplest and most direct way is to simply explain that it is too early in the relationship for you to consider sex and that you need more time before taking this next step. If this is not effective and the man objects, then you must decide whether to stay with or drop this man.

Be Clear about Your Objectives

These four stories exemplify the concept of being clear about what you want, but taking decisive action too quickly.

Doreen went on a first date with Mike, whom she found totally captivating. As the evening proceeded, Mike made the comment that more than anything, he wanted to get married and move back to his birthplace in the country. Doreen, a high profile lawyer in a big city, knew for a fact this would not work for her and did not probe his statement further. She already had decided not to go out with him again. She made an early decision not to waste her time with what appeared to her to be a dead end. This was potentially an error, because she will never know if he really meant what he said or indeed followed through on this dream.

In another first encounter gone awry, Chris, a divorced man, and Mary, who was somewhere over fifty and had no children, met for lunch one afternoon. She told him her dream was to adopt several children from underprivileged countries around the world. To Chris, who had raised four sons and had just finished paying for the youngest son's graduate school program, this sounded catastrophic. But he remembers Mary fondly as one of the most attractive and vivacious women he ever met. In this case, Chris was totally convinced Mary was going to follow through on her dream and decided not to test the veracity of her beliefs. He did not call her again.

Sam likewise shot himself in the foot while sharing his dream with several women he had recently met. He talked with great passion about taking a year off and sailing around the world. While, in all reality, he would probably never do this, his desire came across as so intense that several new encounters in his life chose to bow out, knowing this was something they would never be interested in doing.

Brian constantly remarked to others that he was looking for a sophisticated businesswoman who would join him in his busy social life. Two years later he married a woman who was very warm and caring, was interested in staying home, working in her garden and who loved to cook. Women may say, "I want a man who likes to dance and walk on the beach," yet marry a man who does neither.

The moral of these stories for men and for women: Communication on the first date is important, but one misstatement may end the potential for a subsequent relationship. However, if you are with a person for whom you feel a strong attraction, don't allow one particular statement or idea to scare you off. Many first encounters warrant a second chance. Only then can you get to know someone well enough to evaluate whether such dreams and aspirations have a good chance of becoming reality or are just cherished fantasies.

When In Doubt, Pretend You Are a Politician

Libby, who had been single for over ten years, made this statement to a first date: "There are just no good men out there." Her date, Paul, considered himself to be an average guy and therefore felt he probably would not be able to please her either. He decided she would not find him interesting and did not ask her out again. Many men will take such a statement to mean they are inadequate, even though the woman is obviously not talking about them.

Another error that both male and female newcomers to the midlife dating game often make is engaging in negative conversation. A long dialogue on why their last relationships failed or how unlucky they have been in finding someone with whom they would really like to spend time is not useful in procuring a second date.

You should be forthright if your date asks, "What happened in your last relationship?" This is actually a normal and frequently asked question. You should answer it honestly. Just don't take it as an opening to dwell for an extended time on how awful the relationship was or, even worse, how you are still trying to get over it.

As difficult as it may be, you must behave as though you have been successful in handling a hurtful relationship. Projecting distrust or the feeling that you are afraid to take a chance with a new relationship, because of prior bad experiences, makes finding someone new extremely difficult.

If you have been hurt, it is okay to share your method for healing or simply tell someone that, in fact, you are over the past and have moved on. You may want to discuss how you went through a divorce recovery program and found it very useful. If someone does not relate or have empathy for your past counseling or personal self-help programs, you clearly know they are not on your wave length. People who have been through counseling or relationship workshops often start a new relationship on a different level, with more sensitivity towards others.

Be Careful about Discussing Money and Status

A topic that tends to bug both sexes is blatantly blunt discussions about money. A woman who discusses how much she or one of her friends paid for this item or that dress or how skiing in the Alps is something she can't do without or, even worse, how her alimony just does not cover her expenses, often is very intimidating to men. It is fine if it is a woman's goal to let the man know she is seeking someone of substantial financial means. However, this line of conversation is more likely to give a man the idea he is next in line to support her expensive tastes. If finding a financially well-off man is not your priority, then money is probably a good topic to avoid. Men who blather on endlessly about how much money they have, their newest status toys or, conversely, how poor they have become after their divorces are equally as obnoxious to women as the avaricious woman is to a man. That is why money should be a taboo subject, at least in the beginning. Reminders of material possessions by either men or women are counterproductive. A number of women in our study also advised that it is not a good idea to talk a lot about the success of a former husband. Similarly, men bragging about the beauty or talent of their former wives will not make their dates feel particularly special.

Age: How Important?

Our study validated the fact that both men and women alike date people who are older and younger than themselves. What was surprising is that almost 20 percent of the women stated they had dated younger men and many men indicated they were willing to date older women. When asked what the difference in age was in their relationship, 86 percent of the men stated they were the older partner by an average 8.6 years. The women said 81 percent of their partners were older, with the average being 5.1 years. This means 19 percent of the women have had relationships with younger men and 14 percent of the men with older women. This is a far cry from past eras when most people married with only one or two years difference in their ages. It also shows that the myth that most men are searching for relationships with much younger women is untrue. While some men may initially try to date much younger women, without money, power or fame, they probably aren't going to be successful.

Dating Younger Men

One of the great equalizers of the sexes that has evolved over the past couple of decades is the widespread social acceptance of women dating younger men without condemnation or criticism. In fact, in today's world, most women who date younger men receive accolades from friends. Some women now date men who are substantially younger and the newspapers and television are full of celebrity older woman/younger men stories. This is the "age is just a number" mentality and is a part of a burgeoning "living in the moment" philosophy, which dictates that you should just go with what seems comfortable today and not spend an undue amount of time worrying what it all means. To reiterate the basic theme of this book—the boat is leaving the dock for what may be the last time—it behooves you to be on it.

Women, if you find a mutual attraction with a younger man, go ahead, have the experience. You can have a date or two and discover his maturity level, his qualities, and whether or not he can fit into your life and you into his. Keep things in perspective, don't let the long-term ramifications of such a relationship get in the way…and enjoy yourself.

Dating Younger Women

The reverse situation, men dating younger women, has been more the norm historically and traditionally. The unfortunate fact is that many older men are more likely to date younger women. Many men, particularly finding themselves single after twenty or more years, feel entitled to return to their youthful days and try to date the younger women they missed out on while they were married. Women don't have much sympathy for this attitude, but it is a phase many men go through.

Ellis described his relationship with a woman twenty-five years younger. He said it lasted about a year and summed it up by saying, "My older friends (my age) were a bore to her and her friends were not knowledgeable about topics that interested me. At the beginning and when we were alone, we had a great time, but I learned you cannot live in a vacuum."

The participants in our study made interesting comments about the age factor in dating. Men stated they would date someone three years older to twenty years younger. Women, on the other hand, said they would date someone fifteen years older and ten years younger. These responses assumed that the dating relationship became serious and permanent.

Don't Panic and Don't Get Discouraged

The key to positioning oneself in the midlife dating experience is: Don't panic. Look at the process as a game to be enjoyed. It can be a lot of fun, despite the fears or trepidations you may harbor. Use the time after a relationship break up as a positive experience to grow and then slowly get back into the dating world. While mature people tend to rely on their initial reaction on a first encounter, there is something to be said for not letting one misstatement deter you from a second date, particularly if the chemistry is strong. Granted, you may have to change some pre-conceived attitudes and you may have to hone your social skills, but all in all, being in the game beats the alternatives. Do you have a better plan?

Quiz – Chapter 6

So you are beginning to have some interesting dates. Are you learning the importance of positioning yourself and good communication skills? This quick quiz will help you evaluate where you are in this process. Please rate yourself:

10 points for a "yes"; 5 points for an "undecided"; 0 points for a "no"

Ranking   **Question**

_____ 1. I am clear about my objectives and know what I want.

_____ 2. I am comfortable discussing sex with my date and, when asked, I can enunciate my beliefs.

_____ 3. When I am on a date, I do not dwell on the reasons my last relationship failed.

_____ 4. I don't take everything my date says at face value and I am getting better at reading between the lines.

_____ 5. I keep the discussion of money to a minimum.

_____ 6. I recognize that dating someone who is more than twenty years older or younger than me has a low chance of success.

_____ 7. I am creating a network of interesting friends for social activities.

Scoring

70 – 60 - You are a master at positioning and communication.

50 – 30 - You recognize that you need a little work. This is the first step toward success.

20 – 0 - Go out with people you admire and work on improving your social skills.

CHAPTER 7

Internet Dating, Dating Services and Personal Ads

"It took me over a hundred and fifty Internet dates before I finally found a perfect relationship."

Ed

The majority of the people in our study reported they had either tried or investigated meeting people through the Internet, dating services and/or personal ads. Most people told us their experiences were basically good and the positives outweighed the negatives, but thus far, these experiences had not led to long-term relationships. Many reported they met interesting people, some of whom became good friends. One reason these mostly positive experiences occur is because there is an opportunity to check out the person thoroughly beforehand and take reasonable precautions. One general recommendation was made, especially for women. The first meeting should always be held in a neutral location such as a coffee shop, restaurant or other public place.

There is another major benefit of the Internet, particularly for women. Some dating services and matchmakers have a very low inventory of men over fifty. Even worse, they may have a low inventory of men of any age. Internet sites can fill the need to locate interesting and available men.

According to an analysis by Jupiter Media Metrix, over twenty million people have enrolled in the top five Internet dating sites. That's a significant number. More importantly, these people are not just concentrated in the big cities; they are in rural and suburban areas as well. Five of the top Internet dating services report a combined influx of just over 250,000 new registrations per week! That's a million or more per month and the numbers are growing, not declining. With this many people becoming involved, the Internet could be just what you need.

It's Fun and It's Confidential

While 11 percent of our male respondents reported success in meeting someone on the Internet, a smaller percentage of women reported finding someone. Many in our study commented, however, that some of their friends are reluctant to use high-tech methods to meet people as they believe the Internet is used more by a younger group. In actuality, the Internet services report that a significant percentage of their enrollees are over fifty. Two female friends of Mason and several of Nancy's friends have become engaged within the last year using the Internet and at least a dozen others we know about have found wonderful relationships.

There are a couple of caveats about Internet dating, however, for both men and women. People, particularly those in their middle years or older, may lie about their age or their weight. This is due to two of the basic human nature problems of dating: Many women want men close to their own age or older and men frequently tend to want younger women. This is not necessarily a big deal, since it is the person, not his or her age (at this point in your life) who will be attractive to you. Since you can e-mail back and forth for as long as it takes to make you comfortable with the person, having one meeting will do no harm. Even if all of the statistics are not as represented, who knows what will happen when you actually meet?

If You Try It, Be Truthful

Many people post pictures on Internet dating services, however, some do not. Men and women who do sometimes have a tendency to use pictures that are somewhat out of date. The actual physical appearance of the person is clearly something that will be revealed if you have a date. It may or may not matter to you, but don't be surprised if the person you meet looks different from the person in the photograph!

Our study's experienced Internet daters say that if you don't post your photo your chances of getting a response drop dramatically. As one veteran of the Internet stated, "Without a photo, you are history before you start." Therefore pictures are critical, usually sooner rather than later. You should always insist that you see a picture of the person you are corresponding with before you have that first meeting. If he or she hasn't posted a photo request one in an E-mail message.

Some people take exception to the picture idea. They want complete anonymity on the dating sites for business and safety reasons. If this is your concern, just state in your bio that a picture will be sent in a return E-mail to verify the fact you are acceptable and humanoid. Bear in mind, you are initially communicating through E-mail and remain totally anonymous until you decide to reveal yourself to the person with whom you have established contact. Neither men nor women should give their name or phone number until they feel confident they want the other person to have this information.

The power of a picture should not be underestimated. One woman in our study shared a great Internet story. Her daughter, Patty, posted her picture on an Internet dating site. The only picture she had, however, was a family portrait also showing her sister and mother. An older man visiting the site thought Patty was too young for him, but e-mailed her to inquire about her mother. After convincing her mother to give it a try, Patty gave him her mother's E-mail address. When they got together, it was love at first sight! They have now been together for two years and Patty's mother told us she had met her true soul mate.

Ask All the Right Questions

There is one potential problem with Internet dating of which women need to be aware. Some married men frequent the Internet dating services looking for women with whom they can have sexual encounters. You can smoke out these types by asking some simple key questions before agreeing to meet in person. Where do you live and what is your home address? What is your home phone number? Be alert to cell phones and ask if that is the type of number you are being given. You also should know where a potential date works and what he does. If you get excuses for any of these easy questions, you have an indication this is a man you should not meet. Of course, if you meet him and go out more than once, the easiest way to determine an imposter is to simply see what he does on a Saturday night. If you are not the date, someone else is!

It Really Works!

A big advantage of the Internet is that it is basically inexpensive. For just a few dollars a month you can have access to literally thousands of people.

Many men and women make it almost a job; some have had more than one hundred dates in a year looking for the right person. Ed, a San Francisco bachelor who is forty-nine years old, subscribes to three Internet dating services in his quest for what he considers his ideal woman. He is not just trying to meet and have sex with a lot of women. He truly wants to meet a woman for a permanent relationship. Unfortunately, he often finds himself rejected by women he considers his ideal. Ed does not even try to correspond with a woman who does not have her picture posted and his attitude is fairly common behavior by those who participate in Internet dating.

Presumably, with devotion to his task, Ed will soon find Ms. Right. With over one hundred and fifty dates during the two-year period he has been using the Internet, Ed has found the vast majority of the women he has met to be very interesting. While the majority were not right for him, some have become his good friends. Ed, a vice-president of a telecommunications company and a man with a lot of interests and outside activities, remains a firm believer in the value of Internet dating for making wonderful new friends and to find his future partner.

Since writing this initial story on Ed, there is an update. He found a woman through an Internet dating service and they have been dating for five months. According to Ed, he instantly knew she was his true love. They are perfectly matched, they never argue and they agree on almost every subject to the extent that they even finish one another's statements. This total compatibility led them to make the decision to buy a condominium together. You may say, "Wow! That is fast. Five months is too short to make that kind of decision." Maybe so, but making quick, firm decisions is one of the advantages of being a mature age; you have experienced much, have learned from your mistakes and can now act quickly with a reasonably high degree of confidence in your decision.

Using the Internet like a detective, which we discussed earlier, should be re-emphasized. One woman in our study, Kay, told of meeting a handsome, ultra-smooth man at a cocktail party in San Diego. He came on very strong and, with some trepidation, she agreed to go out with him the following weekend. During the week, she looked up his name on an Internet search engine and found a news item that said his real estate broker's license had been revoked for "a consistent pattern of dishonesty." Needless to say, Kay cancelled the date and threw away his card. The lesson: Use technology to check out any new person, because you never know what you may find. On the positive side, you may find the individual is a well-recognized figure in his or her industry and you can look forward to a very interesting first date.

An Unlikely but True Success Story

Gary, a sixty-seven-year-old business executive who had little time to meet new women, subscribed to an Internet dating service and within four weeks was corresponding with a woman named Christina from Peru…yes, Peru! Gary and Christina e-mailed and talked on the telephone for approximately six weeks, getting to know one another and each other's likes and dislikes.

The intellectual match seemed perfect to Gary and he flew to Peru for a vacation to meet Christina. They spent ten days together, during which time they found they had even more in common. The net result of this Internet match is that she is flying to San Francisco for a three-month stay. Gary believes Christina will end up staying forever.

Now, there is no question that meeting people and dating them over long distances is not the norm. Many of you reading this book will say, "That's just crazy behavior. I don't want to get involved with someone from another country." It is important to keep in mind, however, that "nothing ventured, nothing gained" is the underlying motto of the new world of midlife dating. There is no question this long-distance situation will not be duplicated by most men and women. But it is an example of a successful meeting that would not have been possible without the Internet and would also not have happened had either Gary or Christina not been willing to take a chance.

Let's look at the flip side of this trip and say Gary had flown to Peru with the result that he and Christina did *not* get along. What would be the net result for Gary? Well, he got to see Peru, a country he had not previously visited, he had a new experience, he had an interesting native guide to show him around, but he didn't find true love. Even if romance didn't blossom, the trip certainly had a positive side. A key to midlife dating is that you must have a positive attitude at all times, even when an initial date or encounter is not a success.

Important Tips

Here are a few tips gleaned from people who have years of experience sifting through the virtual pages of Internet dating sites. Also included are some comments writer Ron Geraci made in an article he wrote on Internet dating for *Men's Health* magazine:

> —**Have a catchy code name.** Code names can attract attention and convey something unique or interesting about you (i.e., "Successful and Creative," "Sings in Shower," "Ballroom Dancer," "Tennis

Ace"). This approach may not appeal to everyone, but it gets attention and it gives others a small insight about your personality. However, choosing an overly sexy name is not a particularly good idea.

—**Create an interesting profile.** This is the next step after selecting your Internet name. According to Geraci, he revised his profile sixteen times before he finally got it right. His advice is to study the profiles of other men or women. Your bio should be interesting and breezy. It probably should *not* state you are a magna cum laude graduate of Yale or Oxford (whether it is true or not)—unless you want to weed out any insecure people (a valid reason, which many people feel is desirable for them). Your bio should be about what you like to do on dates and what you are looking for in a dating relationship. You may want to use our survey results to focus your thoughts and gain an insight into what the opposite sex is seeking.

—**Do not sound needy.** Your bio should not sound like you are desperate for a relationship. Many women have disclosed that they love to read bios out loud within their group of friends to see who sounds the most desperate and/or ridiculous. Writing something like "I was married for thirty years and now I'm really lonely and I need to get out of the house" does not tell potential dates anything except this person is badly in need of a life.

—**Include a picture.** If you are new to Internet dating, you need to have a picture taken that will present you at your best. It may be tempting for women to show a lot of cleavage and black lace, but you will appear to be trying too hard. Men should not try to look funny (*being* funny is great; you just don't want to look funny). One woman found a man who posted a picture of himself in a court jester hat (the pointy kind with the little bells). Needless to say, unless there is a woman who is obsessed with the Motley Fools or one who is reading the Internet in Braille, this get-up is not going to attract a whole gaggle of quality women.

—**Explain yourself.** Tell people why you are doing this, for example, "I'm new to the city," not "I just ended a ten year relationship, moved and want to restart my life with someone nice."

—**Write intelligently.** The first impression you make on others in this game is with your writing. Lana is a Harvard graduate with an MBA from Stanford. She stopped dating on the Internet because she felt as though all the men on the dating service were totally illiterate. Have spell check placed on your e-mail so you will not be misjudged from the start. If you are not a good writer, have a friend proofread your bio.

—**Try to add humor.** Be positive about what you do and be clever in your description of the person you are looking for. If you're a woman, don't say you are looking for a man with a high income (men don't want to be wanted for their bank accounts and if you're a man, don't talk about the physical attributes you want her to possess (women will think you are scum if you comment on wanting a woman with large breasts). Even though you may be looking for these qualities, use a little restraint in your presentation. Remember, meeting and dating via E-mail changes a lot of perceptions about what people want and don't want. Your virtual personality, smarts and personal style *do* make a difference when communicating through the written word. You get to know the essence of the person well before your first actual meeting.

—**Respond intelligently.** When you reply to someone, say something about his/her profile that interested you; don't just send an E-mail saying, "I'd like to meet you." Add commentary such as, "I enjoy golf and hiking, too."

—**Show good etiquette.** If someone goes to the trouble of writing to you, write back. A simple "Sorry, you do not meet my criteria" will do. It is a fact, however, that most people do not do this, so don't take it as a negative if you don't get a response.

Success Requires Effort

One man in our study, Peter, told us he made finding Ms. Right the number one priority in his life. With the help of an Internet search, he set his dating parameters: geographical locations (with fifty miles), education (college degree or higher), age (fifty to sixty) and hobbies (outdoor activities). He was a successful business executive and had a bio that sounded down to earth and sincere. Over two hundred women responded. He set aside three hours each day to call and make coffee dates. Some days he saw as many as three women. On contact number 193 (don't laugh), he met his perfect woman and it was mutual. They have been together for over a year. A lot of trouble? Not if finding the perfect person is your number one goal in life. Peter is convinced he and his new love would not have met otherwise.

Try a Dating or Introduction Service

If you don't want to use the Internet, dating services are another alternative to meet new people. Participants have been pre-screened by someone at the dating service and you will have a basic understanding of their backgrounds before you meet. Two general problems with dating services are that they may cost significant money up front (the good ones) and many of the dating services have more women than men as subscribers. If you are a man this is good news; if you are a woman you may find you do not get matched with as many quality men as you anticipated.

Women should ask any dating service how many men they have signed up in the desired age group. Some of the dating services may enlist men and not require them to pay because of the dearth of men enrolled. This is not a bad thing, since these men tend to be high quality, interesting men. Although this is one of the most controversial methods of meeting others and a lot of people feel it has not worked for them, many others have found it very successful. If you can afford it, established, quality dating services are very worthwhile.

A Consequence of Not Being Truthful

Laura, a woman in our study, told us about her experiences with a dating service. Laura is very attractive and in great shape at sixty. New to dating services, she decided to look for a man age fifty, listing her age as the same. She "found" Edward and they hit it off in every possible way. According to her they were soon in the best emotional and sexual relationship she has ever had.

After four months, Laura got up the courage to tell him her real age. She said, "He was furious that I had lied and told me he could never trust me. I never saw him again after that awful night." Clearly, lying didn't work. Honesty really mattered to Edward. So lie at your own risk. However, of all the people who reported they too had lied, when they finally revealed their true ages, it didn't matter to the other people. Edward may have overreacted, but it devastated Laura.

Yes, Personal Ads Also Work

The third alternative, personal ads in major city newspapers or magazines, is also a reasonable approach to meeting new people. The downside is that you have to do all of your own screening and you don't usually get to see a picture of the person to whom you are talking on the phone. The good news is you can get some idea of a person's personality by just listening to the recording you will hear when you answer his or her ad.

If you like the sound of the recording, all you have to do is tell the person something about yourself, which should be as interesting as you can make it in a few sentences. Be sure to leave your phone number for a call back, which they may or may not do once they hear your voice and what you have to say about yourself. If you connect on the telephone and the conversations are pleasant and you feel comfortable with the person, you can then suggest a public location for an initial meeting. If you both have E-mail, you should exchange pictures.

In This Case, Your Voice Is Your First Impression: Make it Interesting

Dana, who lives in Philadelphia, decided personal ads would be a good way to meet men. Although she heard the recordings of several interesting men and left messages, none of them called her back. Her problem? She was totally insecure about herself and in her message came across as a needy woman with low self-esteem. She had few close female or male friends and was therefore unable to discuss her dilemma with people who might have helped. She lost hope and felt she would be unable to meet another man with whom she could have a relationship. Her attitude was, "I'll never find a man who wants me."

The problem was she truly believed this, which caused her to seem very unsure of herself when she recorded her message. She came across as too needy and too anxious and, when she did not hear back after her initial call, she would call again. In short, she was driving any potential man away. Fortunately her best friend talked to her about this dilemma. "Get your life in order, go find some women friends, start doing other activities around your house and stop obsessing about finding a man."

Dana steeled her resolve and did just that. Within six months her attitude was entirely different. She was able to say, "If I find a man, that's great. If I don't, that's okay, too. I am having a wonderful life with my three new friends, traveling and going to dinners, my job is very fulfilling and I love doing things in my garden." She is still answering ads and, with the new self-confidence she exudes, she is getting called back. And if they don't return her calls, she no longer calls them back. But guess what? Most of them call her back.

Why Not Try It?

If you are not meeting quality people in your day-to-day life, you can take matters into your own hands and search for that perfect person using the Internet, dating services, or personal ads. These services will allow you to screen out many undesirable people and let you concentrate on your desired age group, educational background, hobbies, appearance and geographical location. And with over twenty million people out there using the Internet, what are you waiting for?

Quiz – Chapter 7

Do you have an entrepreneurial personality that will let you take advantage of Internet Dating, dating services and personal ads? It's fun and it's confidential! This quick quiz will help you evaluate if this is a good idea for you. Please rate yourself:

10 points for a "yes"; 5 points for an "undecided"; 0 points for a "no"

Ranking	Question
_____	1. I am willing to use Internet Dating, dating services and personal ads.
_____	2. I have/would put my picture on an Internet dating site.
_____	3. I understand the basic rules and would meet someone for the first time in a public place.
_____	4. I do not sound needy in my bio.
_____	5. I have actually answered ads and have arranged a meeting.
_____	6. I do not worry about the types of people I may meet, because I know I can do an adequate job of screening.
_____	7. I have been successful using one of these methods and have had more than one date with the same person.

Scoring

70 – 60 - You have an entrepreneurial spirit and sound ready to try one of these approaches.

50 – 30 - You have a more cautious nature and could take a little more risk.

20 – 0   - Something is holding you back. Try it and see what good things will happen!

CHAPTER 8

Turn Rejection Into a Positive

"Rejection is a part of life—we just need to learn to bounce back quickly,"
Joy

Everyone needs to learn that rejection is okay, regardless of when it occurs. Rejection is not the same as being put on an "enemies" list (unless you have acted very badly)—it merely says you are not the other person's type for a permanent relationship. So don't badmouth the person to others or make inappropriate comments to them: it has no bearing on the relationship's outcome and reflects poorly on you.

Don't Obsess about Being Rejected

Don't take rejection personally. "It is a part of life," as Joy, a woman in our study told us, "you just need to learn to bounce back quickly." In fact, in some ways, it can even be good for you. If it is early in the relationship, it saves you time and can allow you to refocus on other opportunities. Why waste time when there is no potential for a good outcome?

We and our study members know hundreds, if not thousands of rejectees who were connected to others who are more their types by those who rejected them early in the dating cycle, but realized they were good matches for their friends. Remember, everyone has friends of both sexes and they talk to them about their dates. Sometimes people are quite graphic in describing an offensive date. Leave a good impression on your date even if you have just been politely rejected, because he or she might introduce you to someone interesting.

Keep Your Composure. Information Is Not a One-way Street.

Jack knows more about many of his male friends' social lives than they would ever suspect. Because he remains friendly with almost all of the women he dates, they frequently tell him amazing things about men they know. The women shared stories about sexual aggressiveness, poor manners, bad attitudes and macho behavior. Both men and women should never believe they are in the clear when they sever connections with others. How they've behaved in the past may affect their futures, since the individuals they may someday be interested in may have heard about their poor past behavior.

Mason believes that when women hear stories from other women about men, they automatically believe them to be true and that there is little margin for recovery. So be aware, men—you never know when your past may haunt you. This may be a big change from your early years of dating when you may have jumped from one woman to another without regard to what they thought about you. Women are not isolated islands of information. They communicate and can help you or hurt you in your social endeavors. This same advice applies to women acting poorly toward men, but it is a less prevalent occurrence since men seem to have more of an ability, Mason feels, to ignore comments from other men regarding women.

Jim, for example, thought he was making great progress with an elegant woman named Norma. He finally got around to suggesting they should have a date. She looked at him with a semi-incredulous look and said, "Jim, I can't go out with you. I know your ex-wife and I am friends with two of your former girlfriends."

Jim was stunned she would have so much information about him and was literally speechless. In this increasingly small world, there is no such thing as anonymity when you are involved in the midlife dating game. However, all was not lost. Within two weeks, Norma called and fixed him up with a woman she felt would be a good match for his personality.

Rejection Happens. Get Over It!

Women often seem to take rejection in a very personal way and need to learn to toughen up a bit, because, frankly, it's part of the game. Frequently women feel that any sort of rejection by a man is a total repudiation of their being and react with either feelings of hurt or resentfulness. Men seem to have a slight advantage in this area, having experienced rejection on several levels in their careers, businesses or throughout their early years of dating. It is simply a part of everyday life and means "Okay, it's time to move on." A woman needs to take the attitude that her rejector can become a good friend and, because he recognizes she is an interesting person, may introduce her to one of his friends.

The Disappearing Man

Finally, there is the rejection phenomenon of the disappearing man that seems to occur to women with some regularity. This form of rejection is particularly hard to comprehend. In this scenario, you are dating a man for anywhere from one to six months with some regularity (twice a week for example) when without any notice or warning, he suddenly stops calling. This type of rejection is a little more difficult to understand and deal with, since everything appears fine and then there is nothing at all.

Possibly he had another woman he was dating who simply won out (you may have been the "backup," which we will describe in another chapter) or he met another woman who seemed more interesting to him. This happens all the time and, although it can be very disheartening, you can't let it get you down. Calling him will not bring a satisfactory conclusion (since as you probably know by now, many men are notoriously bad at conversations that involve emotion or feelings) and, in fact, he is not likely to have any explanation that makes sense or that he is willing to talk about. So as much as you may want to have some closure and make the call—don't. It will just make you feel worse than you do.

Darlene had been dating the "perfect man" for four months. Every time they were together, he described his close relationship with his grown children and his business associates and told her he wanted her to meet them soon. She was really looking forward to this. He also described his favorite vacation places and suggested they go there in the near future. She agreed to go. Then he told her he was going away on business for several weeks. Weeks passed without so much as a phone call from him. Darlene eventually read in the society column of the local newspaper that he was engaged to a well-known socialite. She was devastated. He had rejected her without having the courtesy or courage, as the case may be, to tell her about the other woman.

Several women told similar stories. One commented, "The next time a date says he wants me to meet his family and friends, I will put his feet to the fire and say, 'When?' If he won't set a time, then I will know it was a ploy."

Leave with Style

Both men and women who want to end their relationships should have the courtesy to tell the other person involved. Simply say that you no longer believe you can pursue a relationship, instead of just disengaging without a word. This can be a simple telephone call to say, "I'm sorry, but I don't think we have enough in common to continue this relationship and I don't want to waste your time," or a more elaborate lunch or dinner date with a discussion of why the relationship will not be fruitful. This is very hard for most people and although it is certainly the right thing to do, you need to recognize it may not happen.

Tony shared what he considers his ultimate rejection story. According to him, he is an excellent tennis player and met Suzanne, who was not. She gave him a huge rush and invited him to play with her in all of her exclusive club tournaments. He gladly obliged, since he was smitten with her and wanted to spend time getting to know her. But after six months, as fall arrived and her tennis league ended for the season, Suzanne was suddenly "unavailable." Abruptly, she stopped seeing Tony all together. He soon heard she was seeing a ski professional and skiing almost every weekend. She disappeared from Tony's life without explanation and moved on, which is exactly what Tony was forced to do.

Learn to Bounce Back Sooner, Not Later

Every one of us has been rejected at least once, if not several times. This is simply a part of life. Some people take it hard and never seem to get over it. Others move on with great resilience. We hope you will learn to bounce back quickly.

Since you are now on your way to becoming a self-assured and confident individual, rejection should not be an issue worth thinking about. Rejection is simply a transitory event and, once it happens, it is already history. Just forget it and move on...don't look back. Seize the opportunity to enjoy your independence without remorse.

Quiz – Chapter 8

This could be the time in your life to look rejection squarely in the face and learn to deal with it. Where are you in this important concept? This quick quiz will help you evaluate just how ready you seem to be. Please rate yourself:

10 points for a "yes"; 5 points for an "undecided"; 0 points for a "no"

Ranking	Question
_____	1. I have been rejected before and I am learning to deal with it.
_____	2. I can shrug off rejection and not obsess over it.
_____	3. When I have a date that has ended poorly, I do not spread negative stories about him or her.
_____	4. I would never just disappear from a relationship.
_____	5. I can have a mature discussion with the opposite sex and explain why I need to end a relationship.
_____	6. I am resilient and try to bounce back quickly.
_____	7. After a relationship ends, I do my best to remain self-assured and confident.

Scoring

70 – 60 - Your compassion and maturity is evident.

50 – 30 - You are on the verge of understanding that rejection has been, and will continue to be, part of everyone's life.

20 – 0 - Tell yourself ten times a day that at some point everyone gets rejected. But don't ignore the potential need for professional help in boosting your self-esteem.

PART 2

The Middle Game:
So Now What?

Introduction

The Middle Game is the point at which you have had a number of dates, you feel comfortable with the other person and you are contemplating taking the relationship to the next level of commitment. You have qualified the other person as a potential "keeper" and now want to establish a deeper connection.

In backgammon, this Middle Game is the most critical. Most errors are made during this period, which is the time when many alternatives must be considered in every move. The mature tournament player uses superior knowledge to gain advantage in making critical decisions.

The Middle Game in dating is also the point where experience and understanding play key roles. Men and women who have a comprehension of their own histories can now begin to understand the background of their potential future mates. This insight can yield huge benefits in evaluating your dating partners during this phase of the relationship. When you were young and green, there was very little past and virtually a non-existent level of experience on which to base judgments about a person of the opposite sex. Now you have this advantage. So use your maturity to gain a win-win situation.

You now have a rich relationship history, and most importantly, you have experience. In most cases you know what attitudes and habits you really like and strongly dislike about the opposite sex. For instance, you know if a potential partner is successful. His or her "potential" is no longer a concern. You don't need to worry about what your children will be like or what kind of father or mother the person will be. You know if she is independent and highly active or a stay-at-home housewife type. The evidence is in! You now have a framework of knowledge to handle the three primary problems of early marriages—sex, money and in-laws. The key to the outcome of the Middle Game is to use the skills and knowledge you have developed during your past relationships to make an intelligent stay or drop decision in new relationships.

In the Middle Game, men may encounter for the first time many independent women in midlife who have ventured into the business world with success. These women will no longer be the submissive housewives that many midlife or older men have become accustomed to as partners. If you are a nineteen-fifties-style man who encounters one of these newly independent women and find that you are interested in someone like this, you will not only need new attitudes, but significantly different behavior.

Your earlier dating experiences could be termed the paleolithic or neanderthal time period versus the twenty-first century. Dating at this point of your life means a whole new approach and requires a totally new mind-set.

In Part Two you will learn the rules of the Middle Game. You will find out what you need to pay attention to in this new era of dating. It includes such important issues as: self-esteem, insecurity and independence. It includes strategies for keeping the romance alive in your relationship and introduces the new concepts of Backups, Returning Veterans and Instant Relationships. This section also discusses what is on everyone's mind, the sex part—do older men and women still want it? It also contains a chapter on dating the glamour people—the powerful, the well known and the very rich. And lastly, it will help you evaluate why someone would want you, as well as why you may want that person.

CHAPTER 9

It's a New Era: Pay Attention

"The well adjusted man does not need to prove he is right about everything. He is comfortable with himself and his ego does not rule his life."

David

Throughout history, men have traditionally been the ones who have pursued and won the woman's heart. Therefore, let's discuss key male traits that women have often had a tendency to overlook or minimize. Clearly some men can have qualities that are not only irritating, but can be severely damaging to women both mentally and physically, if such qualities are not recognized and dealt with early in relationships.

Everyone Now Has a History: Don't Ignore It!

Once you are in the Middle Game and you have both decided to try to make your relationship into something permanent, both men and women need to be aware of any negative characteristics their partner has. For instance, women must not make excuses for, or rationalize men's bad or dangerous qualities, which are, or should be, completely unacceptable in a long-term relationship. If these qualities are just irritating, that's okay, but the really bad ones can involve mental and physical abuse, the need to have complete control over a partner's life, unnatural jealousy, a major ego that dictates that everything he says is correct no matter what the reality, a disregard or lack of respect for woman in general and constant temper explosions. If you are female, these are traits that cannot be ignored at this mature stage of your life. On the other hand, men must also be alert to bad qualities including unnatural dependency, explosive temperament and irrational jealousy in the women they have now decided to consider as long term and possibly permanent partners.

The good news is you can now forget some of the (wrong) reasons you originally made relationship decisions—they are history. Things like pressures and unsolicited comments from your parents or friends to the effect, "This is the perfect man or woman for you." And if your children are older, there is no longer a reason to find a mate because he or she will be a good mother or father for your children. Most importantly, you now know your likes and dislikes in the opposite sex and won't accept unconscionable bad habits or attitudes. You can spot personality flaws and bad behavior in a prospective mate. Hopefully you understand at this point that these qualities are not going to change just because you are now in the person's life.

Some Things Do Change

While making this analysis, it is important to be aware of a little known fact that contradicts what many men and women believe: "People do not change." To some this statement has become almost a holy grail of truth, never to be challenged. There is good news. All is not what is seems; what you may have heard repeated for years is simply not always true. For instance, many Casanova-type men, the Don Juans of some women's pasts have evolved to become loyal and trustworthy partners. For example, Warren Beatty, one of the most notorious womanizers in Hollywood, is now a dedicated husband and father. Don't rush to judge a man's past with other women, though you do need to insure that he has always treated women with respect and without malice.

Some Things, However, Don't Change

Many who are alcoholics are relatively easy to recognize, although you need to be aware of what to look for since they can be very good at disguising this fact. Female alcoholics can be closet drinkers and harder to spot. Pay attention to how much either of you drinks (a lot?) when you are together. Many men and women will deny they are alcoholics and they will most certainly have excuses. They may say they don't really drink *that* much and they really don't need to drink at all—they are just being social. They can be deceptive, however, since they often don't seem to get drunk. True alcoholics often have great capacities to imbibe liquor and often don't exhibit drunken behavior. And you should know many with these failings, even after they have been to counseling, have a high rate of recidivism and may slip back into their old habits.

This does not mean reformed alcoholics should automatically be rejected, but it certainly means you should be on the lookout for excessive drinking. Men and women who have to make excuses for why they drink, or deny they drink that much, are most certainly candidates for a drop. Think about it, if he or she doesn't drink that much, why are they so practiced at denying it? A major reason for divorce stated by women interviewed for this book was, "My husband was an alcoholic."

The Signs Are There. Read Them!

There are lots of other seemingly small things that are actually early warning signs. For instance, driving: Does he or she show real road rage? Not just simple bitching and moaning about traffic, but real action rage like speeding past the offender to cut them off or tailgating them? Or worse yet, getting in verbal or physical altercations with other drivers? Don't you think this has some carryover meaning? If you don't, you are sorely mistaken.

In the case of men, has he gotten physical to the point of making a comment to, or even threatening to punch out, another guy that has looked at, or said "hello" to you? Do you think this is flattering? On the contrary, this is very insecure behavior. The man you want would be happy you are being noticed—he should consider it a great compliment to him and his good taste that other men show an interest in his date.

Nancy once dated a man who was a fabulous ballroom dancer. However, he became furious whenever another man asked her to dance. The next day, the men would call Nancy and say, "What is wrong with this guy?" While he knew all the latest dance steps, his jealous behavior made her so tense that she stopped enjoying dancing with him and quit seeing him altogether.

Does he or she have mood swings that are unpredictable and show a side of themselves that is like a change of personality—a Dr. Jekyll and Mr. Hyde personality? Does he suddenly launch into a diatribe about something relatively minor and take it as an opportunity to level harsh criticism at you, your family or friends? Does she try to isolate you from your family and friends and even the rest of the world? Does he try to make you feel stupid or inferior? These are classic signs of verbal and physical abusers.

When challenged does he or she come back with charm, promises, and an attempt to blame you for the problem? Psychological or verbal abusers often worsen and rarely get better without extensive, intensive therapy—you need to know the signs.

Time for a Drop?

Helen, a fifty-year-old woman in our study and, ironically, a psychologist, was approaching the Middle Game in her relationship with Eric. Her description of their relationship: Most evenings, he was the most charming man she had ever met—until late in the evening. They went out together frequently and many of their activities included parties and hence, alcohol. By the end of dinner it was as if a heavy blanket was wrapping his mind like a cocoon. Instead of being outgoing and witty, he became angry and verbally abusive. His driving became aggressive and bordered on unsafe. At one point, in front of a group of Helen's friends, she suggested that he not have another drink. He yelled at her, told her it was her problem, not his. A friend then drove Helen home and couldn't believe she had put up with this behavior for such a long period. Her friend speculated it was because Helen was lonely and just happy to have found someone who seemed to care about her. Indeed, it was time for a drop.

Staying Until the Bitter End

Adele, a successful businesswoman of forty-six and a mother of four, met a man through a friend who, while not exactly her type, seemed youthful and wholesome. In her words, Simon was boyish, artistic and casual in his attitude. He promoted himself as a religious and fanatically devoted father of four who led an almost "monastic" life. He was also outgoing and very entertaining. These were qualities Adele found appealing. She was lonely, having just ended a seven-year marriage to a man who had been a mental abuser.

Adele told herself that although they had different backgrounds, she was a businesswoman and he was an artist (a starving one at that), she shouldn't limit her options. The compatibility factor seemed very high. They began dating once a week.

After about three months Adele learned there was another girlfriend in the wings. He promised fidelity and did in fact stop seeing the other woman—at least for a while. Over the next two months Simon and Adele spent more time together and the true facts started to emerge. Simon turned out not to be the least bit religious, he was totally irresponsible in raising his children, to the point of neglect, and he became very arrogant and domineering in his attitude toward Adele. He refused to earn a living and was constantly on the verge of being evicted from his apartment, would leave his children alone for days at a time (the oldest was capable of babysitting for the younger ones) while flying to Los Angeles for "workshops," which quickly evolved into parties with his fellow artists.

In short, it became apparent he was a complete flake. When challenged by Adele he immediately reverted to his charming, boyish original self and convinced her he was going to change. He also, however, began to blame her for their problems. His narcissistic attitude began to show on a regular basis and Adele was now in a quandary. She had formed an attachment to a slacker, seemingly devoid of any responsibility towards her and his own children and constantly wanting to exaggerate the truth about everything he had represented about himself when they began the relationship.

It took Adele a year to get rid of Simon and to this day she chastises herself for hanging on until the bitter end and not dropping out of what turned out to be a mentally abusive relationship much earlier. Her dilemma was admittedly an inability to recognize the selfish behavior of Simon much sooner. When she did recognize it, she rationalized to herself that he was really not that bad a person. His charm, perseverance and ability to shift blame to her when challenged clouded her judgment far longer than it should have. Yet she finally extracted herself and has since gained valuable insight as to how to avoid this type of man in the future.

Add Up the Pluses, but Don't Ignore the Negatives

Does your date constantly argue with you and others—even about non-essential points? Does the person put you down when you are alone or when you are around others? As David told us, "The well-adjusted man does not need to prove he is right about everything. He is comfortable with his position and his ego does not rule his life."

How about the woman who constantly wants to know where you have been and what you have been doing in her absence? Do you think that kind of questioning is a concern for your well-being or interest in your life? On the contrary…this may be a woman with great insecurities and one you most certainly want to avoid. Likewise, as a man you should not query a woman about her activities when she is not with you. These are not reasonable inquiries into another person's life.

Is she flexible, will she consider other alternatives than the one she picked, or does she act in a recalcitrant manner and object to any deviation from her plan?

Does he ever comment or brag about business dealings in which he "pulled the wool" over someone's eyes and gained an unfair advantage in some unethical manner? Unethical behavior is indicative of a man who lacks character and it will show up in other ways later.

And the big one…does he or she act as though they truly like the opposite sex? A man or woman who disparages the opposite sex in general or makes constant negative comments about their behavior is not a person who cherishes another. It should be an obvious negative sign, but many people overlook this behavior. Just remember, the person who does not like and show respect for the opposite sex is not going to treat you well in the long run. Wally, a man in our study, commented, "At some point I always try to meet her father; how she treats him is a key to how she will treat me, once the initial rush wears off."

One of the more interesting types of people men and women encounter is the workaholic. This type works as many as twelve hours a day, often six days a week. This leaves little time for a relationship. In the past, men have behaved this way because they were ambitious or just didn't want to go home to a wife and children—which can be chaotic and nerve-wracking to a partner. Women and men should know that at this stage of their lives, when men are with a woman they truly want to see on a permanent basis, they will normally change their workaholic behavior; they want to do things with her and be with her

However, some men and women who form relationships are *both* workaholics or even work together. One woman in our study said, "I am happiest when I am with him, side by side in bed, feet touching, both working on a project which we love. We can work for hours and it is a joy to find someone as involved as I am."

Many relationship teams find the togetherness of work brings them closer together and makes the partnership even more rewarding. This type of bonding most frequently occurs when it is a small business and the man and the woman share the responsibility of managing the company.

Listen to Your Friends. They Care.

Here's a situation almost everyone can relate to: You are dating someone who no one in your family and not one of your friends like. Well, this may not be news you want to hear from your friends, but they probably are right and you probably are wrong. You can rationalize it all you like, but outsiders often clearly see the bad traits you are somehow blinded to—by sex, by an excess of attention or an excitement factor, which is likely far greater than anything you have recently experienced.

Whatever erroneous logic you may use to rationalize your position, you need to pay attention to your friends, children and any other family members who are echoing the same opinion: "Get rid of that guy!" or "Get rid of that woman!" Although once in a great while you will be right, when the consensus of those around you is negative, the probability is you already see the things they are talking about, but are either ignoring these traits or assuming the person will change. *Those traits will disappear once we are married*, you tell yourself. Hah! Think again. Thoughts like, *He (or she) will change once we are committed*, may be the faulty kind of reasoning that got you in trouble before.

The woman's reasoning often goes something like this, "He has friends who are really distasteful to me, he has a very bad temper, he doesn't clean up after himself, *but* he has a really good heart and I know he loves me." Please, please, please don't succumb to this line of reasoning—he is not salvageable and it is only a matter of time before you regret you got involved with this man. Don't do it! Remember the first man you thought you could change and didn't? And then spent endless time regretting what wasn't to be? So what's different now? The answer—*nothing*.

There is a good chance your intuition has already told you this is a bad match, but you are very attracted and, unfortunately, it is often very hard for women to abandon men with whom they've invested a substantial amount of time, particularly if they are "understanding" or "sensitive" or "the sex is just wonderful." Well, listen to your basic intuition—and to your friends. It will lead you to the correct decision.

Men suffer from the same sort of irrationality. "She is a great sex partner, she caters to my every whim, she doesn't get upset with me and she is always pleasant to be around." This is a very appealing scenario—right? So why aren't all of your friends telling you what a great woman she is? Well, you must be missing something. They see it, but you don't. Can they all be wrong? Time to pay attention to the little things you may have been trying to ignore.

You Can't Ignore Subtle Signs of Abuse

There is a serious, often hushed issue that affects roughly 10 to 15 percent of women. That is the problem of mental or emotional abuse that many women have had inflicted on them during the course of a marriage or relationship. Mental abuse by men is an insidious means of controlling women that is often so subtle in its initial stages that women are not aware it is happening to them. Women who have experienced this sort of treatment know it often can totally drain their ability to control their own lives.

Sometimes a writer of fiction can zero in and describe mental abuse toward women in a way that truly speaks to the issue. In Danielle Steel's book *Journey*, a character, a famous psychiatrist, explains: "Abusers wear many hats and many faces." He goes on to describe men who need to control women, who destroy their confidence, who isolate and frighten them, who take away their free will, their reproductive choices, their money, their self-respect. He tells Maddy, the main character, that mental abuse is "...just as painful, just as dangerous, just as lethal, as the kind that leaves bruises."

If you are one of the women who has been a victim of abuse, you probably need professional counseling. However, the first thing you must do is recognize that you have suffered abuse and decide to do something about it. This book is not about solving this serious problem, but we wish to make women who have experienced this negative relationship dynamic be aware that there is truly the possibility of a happy life and a healthy relationship with another man if professional help is sought.

Even with therapeutic help, if you have been involved in an abusive relationship, you will clearly need to address the issue of healing. No one is saying this can happen quickly. It may take years to move beyond a history of these kinds of relationships and begin to trust a man again, but that doesn't mean you shouldn't try. If this book does nothing more than inspire you not to give up, then our message has gotten through. Certainly it is not easy and there are no guarantees, but for the sake of your future, why not try?

Decide if Financial Issues Are Important and Act Accordingly

Harry, a man in our study, was close to making a commitment to Susan. Harry had inherited a great deal of money from his father. Susan remarked one night that she would never sign a prenuptial agreement and became very argumentative and obstinate about the issue (Susan didn't own a home and had few assets). While Harry wanted Susan in his will, he also had a teenage daughter who he felt deserved most of his assets. He saw Susan's reaction as being totally unwarranted and unreasonable and felt this might be indicative of other significant irrational behavior in the future. After a second discussion, which also became heated, he ended the relationship. Was her obstinance an aberration? Or was it the tip of the iceberg? Harry will never know, but he did not ignore his instincts and made an educated guess, because the future was so important.

Self-preservation issues need to be evaluated more closely at midlife and beyond. Rule one is to determine if your current romantic partner is financially self-sufficient or just looking for a meal ticket. As men and women get older, financial stability is often an issue. If neither partner has any substantial assets, or if their assets are more or less equal, then there presumably will be no problem—at least as far as asset ownership. But if one of the partners has substantially more financial assets, there may well be family or other reasons to protect such assets.

First, there is certainly no reason you can't marry or have a long-term relationship with someone even though you know your money is one of the main attractions. It doesn't mean that person can't love you—your financial position may just be a "value added" benefit for the both of you. Many women and a number of men make the decision to marry wealthy partners; this doesn't mean they don't also love them (wealthy men and women can be kind, sensitive and loving, just like anyone else). Financial imbalance can work in relationships.

However, there is a flip side to the financial imbalance and it may exist for either the man or the woman. One of you may have accumulated enough money to live comfortably for the rest of your life supporting your own existing lifestyle, but when it comes to supporting another person in that same lifestyle, the math doesn't work. You may not be willing to add the financial burden of a full-time partner.

If two people are dating and beginning to become serious about one another, yet one seems reluctant to make a commitment, it is possible that his or her concern over the prospect of having to totally support the other person could be the reason. This may be particularly true if there are children to whom the wealthier individual wants to leave his or her estate. If you sense that you are involved in such a situation, you might want to be sure your potential partner understands you would not be a financial burden. This is another area in which a prenuptial agreement can obviate the problem.

Age makes everyone pay more attention to finances—it's one of life's realities. Many people feel, "If we're in love, we can make our relationship work and money will not be a problem." If that is your attitude then maybe this will happen and you will not want to take steps to secure your assets. However, being older is often tempered by the attitude, "I don't want to risk losing what I have, no matter what." This is reasonable, since in many cases, at this stage of your life you have some hard-won financial security. In addition, if money was ever a problem in a previous marriage or relationship, then it probably will be even more so today, unless you and your partner both understand the situation and the possible consequences.

To protect an insecure partner or both partners, you may need to sign an admittedly unromantic prenuptial agreement. However, if everything else is good and you have a lot of things in common, then don't get emotional about a piece of paper and execute a drop decision. The partner who has significant financial resources may want to consider such an agreement. Tackle this problem in a businesslike, logical way, even though you may be emotional about the subject. Money is the number one reason couples disagree. Save yourself and your partner from arguments by settling the way you will handle your joint and individual finances—now.

Always Keep Romance

The romance we discussed in other chapters relevant to the Beginning Game is still relevant in the Middle Game. Now that you have both made a commitment to dating and are in a quasi-relationship (this can be after three dates or thirty dates), the role of romance should accelerate rather than diminish. Some young men use romance in the early days of a relationship to get the girl and afterward forget the meaning of the word. Some young women, mired down in everyday tasks and child-rearing, lose the precious quality of romance.

A very important point for both men and women to remember is to work to keep the romance in their mature relationships. Men: Don't abandon romance just because you now feel you are securely in a relationship. Men historically begin to take women for granted and start to ignore and discard all of the early romantic efforts they made during the Beginning Game. It is important that men do not deteriorate into the old habits of ignoring women's basic requirements for attention and romance.

Dancing: The Ultimate Gesture

One activity which many women and some men consider romantic is dancing. Dancing, for a large percentage of women, is one of the ultimate gestures that says a man cares. The personal ads in newspapers, magazines or on Internet dating services from females seeking males show that a lot of women want men who are interested in dancing. So if a man wants to be responsive to this, he should take his partner out for dinner and then somewhere to dance.

Many large hotels feature small dance floors with live music. This is an ideal romantic setting. Don't take your date to a crowded or loud dance club; go to a smaller, quiet location. Even if you just stumble around, the fact you made the gesture is perceived as important to many women. If you really don't dance well, enroll in a ballroom dancing class, either with a woman you enjoy or by yourself. It will be time well spent.

Gifts: To Give or Not to Give

Men and women will sometimes buy expensive gifts as a way to show their romantic feelings. This is an area you will have to judge based on your own feelings about this sort of behavior. Some women and men find this flattering and a sign of strong emotion on the part of the other person. They accept the gifts as an indication of the person's intensity. On the other hand, some men and women often feel this is too much, too soon and feel overwhelmed with expensive gifts. They feel valuable tokens create too much pressure and they react negatively.

Men and women need to read the other person's feelings on the gift issue before they act with haste and do something that ends up offending rather than flattering. Certainly, as the relationship progresses beyond the Middle Game, this is an issue that disappears, but many at this middle stage may feel uncomfortable until they feel fully committed.

Now Is the Time to Pay Attention

During the Middle Game of the relationship, complications may start to set in and many outside influences start to affect the relationship. Idiosyncrasies begin to appear and make-or-break habits are examined. Clearly this is the point at which a logical person should be making realistic decisions about the relationship. If you had a previous unhappy marriage or committed relationship, you now have the chance to avoid the original error you made.

The Middle Game period is the time when many critical decisions are made which will cause the relationship to go either forward or backward. At your mature stage of life, you should not be saying, "I just want to get married and the flaws I see in the other person can be resolved after we are married." You must not make that fatal error again. This, of course, does not mean you can't settle for someone who is less than the perfect person you envisioned marrying in your twenties. Relationships cannot stay in a middle ground for long. You need to recognize the major characteristics that will eventually doom or make the relationship succeed. Once you have this insight into the other person you can act accordingly and make the stay or drop decision.

Quiz – Chapter Nine

Congratulations! You are now entering the Middle Game and during this time you will need to make many critical decisions as to whether this relationship is an enduring one. Please rate yourself:

10 points for a "yes"; 5 points for an "undecided"; 0 points for a "no"

Ranking   Question

_____ 1. I pay attention to the history of my dates and use this information as an indication of what he or she is like.

_____ 2. I know the signs of an alcoholic and can ascertain if he/she is still drinking.

_____ 3. I would not stay until the bitter end of a relationship when my intuition tells me it is not working.

_____ 4. In the Middle Game, I would expect my partner to spend more time with me, even if he/she is a workaholic.

_____ 5. I listen to my friends' opinions regarding my dates and relationships.

_____ 6. I believe I can clearly recognize the signs of abuse and am mature enough not to be in this kind of a relationship.

_____ 7. I work at maintaining the romance in my relationships beyond just the early stages.

Scoring

70 – 60 - Your eyes are open, and you understand the basic rule of the Middle Game.

50 – 30 - Take a risk, you will find it is worth it.

20 – 0 - You need to become more realistic and observant to create a long-term relationship.

CHAPTER 10

Self–esteem, Insecurity and Independence

"I regained my self-esteem and threw Baxter out of my life."
Sandra

In general, men with healthy minds do not want to date insecure women, nor do secure women want needy men. That said, there are a certain percentage of men and women who actually want partners who totally depend on *them*. A man or woman with low self-esteem, or one who can be controlled, makes life somewhat easier for the other partner, because he or she will do just about anything requested. Needy and insecure people don't make waves and their relationships can become a form of slavery. However, mature people want equal partners whose opinions they solicit and respect.

The Need for Self-esteem Cannot Be Overestimated

Nothing is more important for romantic love than self-esteem. We must first be in love with ourselves; only then can we love another. If we cannot love ourselves, it is difficult, if not impossible, to believe someone else can love us.

High self-esteem gives us the confidence to approach and meet a new person. Since self-esteem first affects our behavior during the beginning phase of a relationship, we asked our survey participants, "When you are initially introduced to or casually meet someone, who do you think selected who?" Some 32 percent of the men stated they felt they had selected the women and 16 percent felt the women had selected them. Over half of the men (52 percent) felt it was a mutual decision. Conversely, 5 percent of the women felt they had done the selecting, with 24 percent feeling the man had chosen them. Seventy-one percent felt it was a mutual selection.

Women with High Self-esteem Can Approach Men with Impunity

The fact that the vast majority of men and women surveyed felt it was a mutual decision to get together would seem to indicate that most people, but particularly women, felt they got together as a result of a normal or chance interaction and did not consider themselves selected. As confirmed by our survey, women have traditionally been reluctant to approach men. A mere 5 percent said they initiated the first contact, while almost one third of men said they were the first to approach a woman. This is not surprising since historically, it has been the man who initiated contact. But today, of course, it is more acceptable (and even recommended) for *either* party to take the lead in making a connection with the opposite sex.

It is in the all-important first meeting and conversation that the quality of self-confidence becomes immediately apparent. Both men and women need a sense of high self-esteem and a sense of security in their own beings to begin the dialogue with a new person which may lead to a fulfilling relationship.

If You Are Strong and Self-Sufficient, It Will Be Obvious

The independence and self-sufficiency you project will convey that you are an emotionally stable person who has adjusted to the good and bad events of life. Once the first date is in process it becomes even more important to project the fact that you possess these qualities. It is important you have a confidence level that allows you to be seen as a potentially equal partner. This is crucial. Otherwise you are doomed to a series of failures and you will not succeed in the Middle Game.

Some emotionally secure and strong people, after the loss of loved ones, can temporarily revert to becoming needy or insecure. If you find yourself in this state for a time, realize that it is to be expected. The heart will heal eventually and you will return to your positive state. However, some individuals may stay depressed for a number of years or, in the worst cases, forever, but again, this is not the norm. Since self-esteem and emotional stability are high on the list of characteristics both men and women desire in a partner, it is important that you cultivate and project these valued qualities. The opinions about this subject were so strong that many added the comment, "I would not even consider dating someone I believe has serious, unresolved emotional issues."

Before the initial meeting with a potential partner, one of your first priorities is to take action to rid yourself of any feelings of low self-esteem you may harbor. To do this, you may want to consult with a counselor so that you can work through your own issues. Do whatever it takes—professional help, group therapy or workshops—to move past these negative feelings and behaviors.

One of Rod's experiences with female insecurity involved a blind date with Gail, who had a bouquet of helium filled balloons and an affectionate card sent to his office before their first date. They had talked on the telephone and she sounded smart and interesting, but when the balloons arrived, his feeling of enthusiasm immediately went to one of trepidation. Why would someone make such a grandiose romantic gesture before meeting? To Rod, what this ploy actually said is that this is a very needy woman who is trying too hard. He went into the date with a very negative attitude and there was nothing that occurred during that evening with Gail which changed his view. This rule is so important that it must be repeated—*don't do things that make you appear obviously needy!*

Women and men with low self-esteem often have the mistaken belief that their worth comes from the opposite sex's attention and affection. Instead of first loving themselves, they turn to others to boost their self-esteem. Their need for a relationship usually causes them to make poor choices and, while it may last for a short time, the relationship will ultimately backfire.

A Dependent Woman

Sandra, a woman in our study, had been married for over twenty-five years when her husband walked out on her to marry a younger co-worker. She told us, "For months, I felt my life was over and then I met Baxter. He came on very strong and we were soon in a relationship. I had never been in a relationship with anyone other than my husband, who I married my junior year of college. I immediately became dependent upon Baxter for almost everything. He even helped me select my clothes.

"Unfortunately, Baxter took advantage and constantly berated me when I failed to do something he wanted. When he threatened to leave me, I begged him to stay. I finally began pulling myself together and the last time he threatened to leave, reality set in and I said, 'Okay, go.'

"He was shocked and said he didn't mean it; this was only a lover's quarrel. Finally, however, I regained my self-esteem and threw Baxter out of my life, but not before I had to put up with a lot of two-in-the-morning phone calls and his knocking on my door at all hours. I may have been the woman of his dreams, a totally dependent and needy person, but it soon became clear to me that I was no longer that woman. It just took me a little while to get my act together and regain my self-esteem."

A Dependent Man

A man who is very insecure and dependent often wants a woman who is willing to take care of him. Such men will ask their dates what they want to do and then let them make all the decisions. Dependent men let women run their lives and are subservient to their every need. The woman is in control and that's the way they want it to be. If you're a woman who is interested in and likes the type of man who needs to be nurtured in this way, then that's great. At least you are now mature enough to recognize you want this type of control. Just as with men who like needy women, there are women who want needy men. Perhaps it's the Florence Nightingale syndrome, the feeling that the man can either be saved or helped through the ministrations of a strong woman. Clearly, if you are a woman with this mind set, then the needy man is for you. However, recognize that this is a co-dependent relationship.

Men who are still in pain and/or recovering from a past relationship will often be especially attracted to a nurturing woman. Such a man needs to be comforted and feel a sense of intimacy. However, once healed, he usually realizes the dependence on which the relationship is based and, as soon as his confidence returns, he too will be ready for a more equal and appropriate relationship. This is one of the primary reasons many women avoid men who have just ended a long marriage or relationship. This attitude may be valid, but women should realize this isn't by any means a universal problem. Those who are recovering will usually be very obvious, but don't reject an otherwise good man for the wrong reason.

Do You Want a Walking Wounded Personality?

Cynthia was a woman Barry desperately wanted to marry, but she decided to marry another man because "he needed her." Cynthia had decided that while she knew Barry loved her and wanted her on a permanent basis, the other man not only loved her and wanted her, but he needed her more than Barry did. Barry did not believe in the concept of "need" as a basis for a relationship and when they parted, he told her so. After a few years with the other man, Cynthia left him and became one of Barry's Returning Veterans, which are described in a later chapter.

Cynthia had learned that having someone need you is not necessarily a proper reason to establish a long-term happy relationship. She discovered she was not a good partner for a needy person, but since she was young at the time she had the mistaken impression that this would solidify the relationship. She also realized she was not good at nurturing a needy personality type. One of the things we learn as we develop experience and move into the midlife dating category is that "need" is not a good reason to create a mature partnership.

Relationship Junkies Are Hard to Spot

The other type of needy person is the relationship junkie. This person (who can be either sex, but is usually male) is like a dog that chases cars—he does not really want to catch one. This is essentially playboy-like behavior, but is different in that, unlike the playboy who knows he does not want the relationship, the relationship junkie is sincere in the belief he wants a real relationship.

The relationship junkie will wine and dine the object of his affection; he will take her on romantic weekends and will profess undying love on the second or third date. However, when the lover reciprocates, the junkie pulls away and pursues the next relationship. This type of man is very difficult for women, since there is no way to ascertain his true intentions. Many of our survey respondents, apparently with experience in this sort of situation, emphasized the importance of learning about the past behavior of any man who comes on very strong at the outset. As we said before, "the big rush" that begins immediately after your first meeting is a red flag that should not be ignored.

The bad news is this is a very difficult man to decipher and the odds of learning his true motives (since he himself believes he wants the relationship) are almost nil. This is in direct contrast to the Casanova-type male who will usually be up front and tell you his intentions and who may well change if he perceives you are truly the right person.

For some people, these are post-divorce syndromes that wear off. For others, it is a permanent state. And yes, this is a bad situation to be in and one everyone would like to avoid. However, life is life, and we all get in the game not knowing what will happen. The only way to avoid this is to totally retreat—

do not date, do not be social, do not be open to new experiences—and we all know what a poor solution to finding happiness this would be.

Learning the Hard Way

Another woman in our study, Patricia, is a hospital administrator in New Hampshire. She began dating Taylor, a surgeon, who worked at the same hospital. From their first date, Taylor came on very strong, telling her they were perfect together and should always be a couple. Patricia thought he seemed very insecure—he called her several times a day on her cell phone, interrupting her work, and sent flowers and other expensive tokens of his affection.

He soon talked her into going away for a weekend (where she thought they had a wonderful time), but, after returning, their relationship dissolved with no forewarning and no apparent cause. Patricia was heartbroken and after a year got engaged to a man who was much more easygoing. When Taylor heard of her engagement, he called and said he had to see her. During dinner, he tried to spark her fantasies once again. The difference this time was that she had the self-confidence to reject his romantic appeal. Luckily, she had the maturity not to get swept up in fairyland again.

The Independent Woman: Are You Sure You Want One?

What happens when a man encounters a truly independent woman? Sometimes they click, other times they don't. Many men often think (and even convince themselves) they want an independent woman, but they may not. Strong-willed women are not prone to taking direction without logic and good reason and they demand that men contribute equally to the relationship. If a man's prior relationships were not like this, it will be very different when he encounters one of these women. Such women have busy and fulfilling lives of their own and may not include their partners in all of their activities.

One independent woman in our study, Marcie, is president and founder of her own company. She makes no apologies for telling everyone that the company comes first in her life. While she told us she wants to find a relationship, she still works ten hours a day, six days a week. She jokingly says she will probably remain married to her career. A relationship with

Marcie could work for a man who is also independent and whose high self-esteem allows him to recognize her outstanding accomplishments and be proud of her.

In short, independent women don't need men in the older, more traditional ways. They may want men in their lives, but they don't *need* them. Men need to be clear in their own minds that they can truly accept independent, strong women. If you are a man who wants an equal partner, but you are used to being king and dominating a relationship, you probably will not be happy with a woman who is truly independent.

The Worst Advice a Woman Can Get

For a man who is used to being in financial, intellectual and emotional control of a relationship, it may be difficult or even impossible to adjust to a woman who is self-sufficient and independent. Many strong women know that men, particularly older men, often have a problem with independent women and fake it and dumb down for a while to get a particular man interested. This is the most absurd advice a woman can get. Even if it worked, can you imagine playing dumb the rest of your life? So if you do decide to implement this strategy, just be sure you know what you are doing and be prepared to live with the long-term consequences. Or, even more disturbingly, what if the guy doesn't figure it out—he's just too dense? Congratulations, you have just married a moron.

Needy or Self-sufficient? Make the Choice

Man or woman, you must decide which is more appealing to you: independent and self-sufficient or controlling, co-dependent and insecure? There is clearly no right or wrong, but the key issue in your mature years is to recognize your *own* needs and then make sure the person you choose as a partner has the qualities that will balance yours, add to the relationship and bring out the best in both of you. When this happens you will be in a win-win relationship.

Quiz – Chapter 10

This chapter helps you to evaluate the person you are and the qualities you feel you need in a relationship. This quick quiz will help you know whether or not you are meeting your goals. Please rate yourself:

10 points for a "yes"; 5 points for an "undecided"; 0 points for a "no"

Ranking   Question

_____ 1. I feel emotionally secure.

_____ 2. I am becoming an independent person.

_____ 3. I love myself and am ready to love another person.

_____ 4. My friends tell me that I do not project an image of being needy.

_____ 5. If I encounter a relationship junkie, no matter how charming, I know I need to move on.

_____ 6. I can deal with and appreciate a truly independent person and not be threatened.

_____ 7. I have identified qualities that are right for me in a prospective partner and I'm looking for a relationship in which I find them.

Scoring

70 – 60 - You are able to deal with almost any situation.

50 – 30 - You understand how to read the negatives in a relationship and you are reacting appropriately.

20 – 0   - Just spend a little more time learning about yourself to gain self-confidence.

CHAPTER 11

Romantic Strategies: Dos and Don'ts

"I have found that cooking a meal can have great romantic significance."

Carl

Romance has traditionally been something favored more by women than men. According to some venerable and legendary wit, "Women want romance and men want sex." This was a common belief for most of history. Today, women still want romance, but men have a better appreciation of the quality romance can bring to a relationship. Older men know that making romantic gestures such as sending cards or flowers and making an occasional call just to say hello is very helpful in winning over women. While it may have been a ploy males used to get sex when they were younger, it is now more frequently a sincere gesture. Women, too, have learned that caring gestures can earn their partners' appreciation.

Women's Romantic Needs

The good news for modern mature women is that they have a far better opportunity for romance from today's more sensitive older men. Sigmund Freud once said, "The great question I have not been able to answer is, 'What does a woman want?'" Well, Sigmund, one significant answer is romance. Midlife and older women now get a new chance for romance from men who have learned the necessity for this important element of a relationship.

This is especially positive since many women in our study emphasized their need for continuing and on-going caring gestures. Small gifts on holidays such as Valentine's Day, the anniversary of a first meeting or other special event show that their partners care. As Jill related, "Small gifts during the year mean much more to me than one major gift once a year. I know he is thinking about me."

Still…Some Men Don't Get It

Laurie, a fifty-year-old Philadelphia woman who responded to our survey, recently met a man she instinctively liked. He appeared smart and charming. There was chemistry on her part and she looked forward to their date. However, their first evening together consisted of his telling her about his accomplishments, what he did and what he liked to do. Not once did he ask Laurie about herself or her interests. At the end of the evening, he walked her to the door and, in Laurie's words, made "a bumbling attempt to kiss me." She rejected the attempt and went inside.

He called again and, because she still felt an attraction to this man, she went on another date, hoping their first had been an aberration. Unfortunately, their second date was a duplication of the first one, more talk about what he liked in a woman with no two-way communication, no questioning of Laurie as to what she thought about or looked for in a companion. In short, there was no communication or sense of romance.

As her date walked her to her door, he attempted to kiss her again and go inside the house with her. Laurie's comment: "What can this man have been thinking? Is his ego so great that he thought I would be interested just because he was a successful businessman?" The result was a clear drop decision by Laurie.

Open Up with Personal Data

While we have emphasized the negative results men bring about by having a preoccupation with their own lives and not listening to women, there is a fair amount of divergence on this issue since sometimes opening up and telling a life story can be just what a woman wants to hear. For the record, most women welcome a deep and personal conversation. However, to many men, conversations often include analytical problem solving and bottom line ideas. For a woman, conversation usually means sharing emotions and inner thoughts.

This difference may be difficult to accept for many men, but it would be worthwhile for male readers to try a simple experiment. On your next date make a concentrated effort to not say a single word about what you do. If your date asks you what business you're in, give a short one or two sentence explanation and then switch to telling something about your past life, such as r childhood stories (remember Clarence?) or talk about your feelings. See what different reactions you get when you open up about personal thoughts and emotions.

Laurie's experience illustrates that an aggressive, insensitive, macho, "I am Mr. Wonderful" attitude rarely works. A man needs to learn to have two-way communication; he needs to express interest in a woman's life, her hobbies, her likes and dislikes. He needs to be able to express his inner feelings and emotions without fear he will be perceived as a wimp. And he needs to learn when to be affectionate and sexual and when it just isn't appropriate.

Men's Needs

Although women crave romance, men also have needs which are important to them. For many it is empathy, companionship, interest in their business lives and leisure time pursuits. For many women, romance comes before meaningful sex, while for many men sexual attraction is primary. Yet most mature men want to know that the women to whom they are attracted share their interests and, most of all, are interested in them.

Daniel told us of one of his negative first date experiences. A woman he had been looking forward to taking out monopolized the entire conversation by talking about the cute escapades of her two children. She didn't ask him a single question about himself or even if he had children. Needless to say that was their first and last date.

Creative Ways to Win Hearts

Many women want communication (real two-way communication), a sense of sharing, intimacy and, needless to say, romance. Mature women understand how fragile and important men's egos are. Voicing attraction and admiration, as well as sharing simple things, gives evidence that a woman is interested in the man himself and not just his success or financial standing.

Carl told us, "I have found that a simple gesture like cooking a meal can have great romantic significance." Many of the respondents in our survey told us, "Sex begins in the kitchen." Just cooking a meal for someone says you care a lot about that person. It has even more significance when a man cooks a meal for a woman. Many men have actually gone to a cooking school, because they felt this was such an important part of romance. If you are a man who can cook even one meal, it's one of the grandest romantic gestures you can make in the early dating stages.

Nancy reflects on one of her most romantic evenings. Her date was a visiting professor from France with little money. She was told to dress informally, then was picked up at four in the afternoon and driven to the top of a nearby hill. A picnic blanket was spread on the ground, and she was offered a chilled glass of chardonnay, a slice of Brie and a chunk of French bread. They had a wonderful discussion about books and plays. And to top it off, there was a perfect sunset. This was a simple date, which was clearly impressive and always remembered.

The Simple Home-cooked Meal

Man or woman, you may not be accomplished in the kitchen, but mastering a few basic recipes will do wonders for your image. It will certainly show a date you care enough to make the effort and while the quality of the meal is basically irrelevant, you might as well try to make it a truly excellent dinner. Even if you are a complete bumbler, he or she will not be put off by your attempt at showing you care.

First, if your date drinks, be sure to serve him or her a glass of good wine. While it is true that many people cannot recognize a very good wine, they can usually tell a very bad wine, so don't try to skimp in this area. Since dry wines are generally perceived to be better than fruity wines by many (and if you are not enough of an expert in wines to defend your choice), just ask for a dry one when you make your purchase.

Serve an appetizer while you are drinking the wine. A considerate host might also have mineral water on hand with a slice of lemon or lime. This attention to detail and extra flair will show thoughtfulness (and is a good fall back position in case your date does not drink). Advice: If your date offers to help in preparation or even in clearing the table after dinner, don't let them—this time. After a few more dates, you might share both preparation and cleanup.

Your ability to be self-sufficient and your desire to have him or her simply enjoy the evening will be greatly appreciated. And remember, anything you prepare (even using packaged ingredients) can be excellent. Do not confuse excellence with complexity and creating the dinner from scratch.

Basically, all you need to do is master two or three basic recipes that will make you look like you are a true cooking professional. Simplicity is the key, as is the ability not to have the meal take forever to prepare. The following suggestions can be prepared with minimal effort and are well balanced and tasty.

The starting point: an appetizer is easy to prepare and works well with the wine. This works while you are in the kitchen both cooking and chatting. You, as the chef, can be cooking while your date is either standing or seated nearby. This will take just a few moments and is a wonderful start to an evening. An appetizer can be as simple as a good cheese and crisp crackers (be sure they are not stale), raw vegetables with a premixed dip you can buy off the shelf or a gourmet frozen hors d'oeuvre that you can prepare in the microwave.

The salad, which can be offered before or after dinner, need not be complicated. The logic of serving salad after dinner, which is the European style, is that the dressing may dull taste buds if eaten before dinner. The salad can be a simple one consisting of fresh mixed greens and one or two ripe red tomatoes with a simple oil, vinegar and spice dressing. Cut the tomatoes into either small cubes or slices and mix with the lettuce. If you want to be more ambitious and show more initiative, you can also add chopped celery, cucumbers, onions, carrots or an avocado.

To make the salad special, after washing the lettuce make sure it is dry before you add the salad dressing. Alternatively, you can now buy lettuce or spinach that has been pre-washed and packaged in airtight bags. Mix the salad dressing with the lettuce and tomatoes or other vegetables when you are ready to eat the salad; do not premix the lettuce and dressing since it will result in a very soggy mixture.

For the main course, pasta is a good option, since it is high in carbohydrates, which will provide quick energy, is easy to digest and is a stimulating (as opposed to a "heavy") food type. The other advantage of pasta as a main course is its ease of preparation, although salmon or chicken recipes are good choices also. Today, more people are into healthy lifestyles which stress eating lighter fare. If you select pasta as the main course, buy imported pasta (100 percent hard durum semolina) that will have more flavor and does not contain the very heavy egg and flour content of the homemade variety that will tend to put your date to sleep after dinner (presumably not an objective). Small pieces of chicken or diced vegetables make a good addition to mix in with the pasta.

You may want to use fresh lemon juice with items you prepare to give them extra zest. For example, lemon juice goes well with any cooked vegetable or potato dish; add it to soups to intensify the flavor; it is also excellent with any fish and it can be an interesting addition to almost any dressing. It goes well over scrambled eggs, should you be cooking breakfast for your date the next morning or meeting early on a Sunday to spend the day together.

After dinner, consider a light dessert such as cookies or fruit or simply serve a liqueur such as amaretto or even a small brandy. If you don't drink, then serve some fresh coffee or prepare an espresso, which will be different and interesting, or offer a variety of teas and biscuits and chocolates.

Last, but not least, is creating the setting for an intimate dinner. The candles, wine and bottled water need to be in place before you start your dinner process. Have softer lighting, a fine tablecloth, napkins (not paper!) and music conducive to an intimate dinner. Fresh flowers will add the perfect touch. You have done well thus far; don't fail to create a totally stimulating and memorable environment. Women often notice what to men are seemingly insignificant and unimportant details; men frequently care more about the overall effect.

Romance Doesn't (and Shouldn't) End

Romance, romance and then more romance—to a man it often seems as though women can't get enough of it. Well, in fact, most of them can't. The basic rule for any man: When in doubt—about anything you may have done to offend your partner or anything you even *think* you may have done—do something romantic! If you are to have any chance at recovery, a romantic gesture is by far your best option. Parenthetically, most men also love a romantic gesture and will respond very favorably when one is made.

The good news for men is they often do a lot of little things they don't consider romantic, but to their surprise, appear to many women as the most romantic things they have witnessed. Yes, men can be romantic by accident! The good news for women is that most men appreciate the caring touch that shows a special effort has been made especially for them. The key, of course, is that it is the little things that make a difference. Use your imagination.

Quiz – Chapter 11

Are you open to romance in a relationship and do you understand the dos and don'ts? This quick quiz will help you evaluate where you are in this important area. Please rate yourself:

10 points for a "yes"; 5 points for an "undecided"; 0 points for a "no"

Ranking   **Question**

_____ 1. I am aware of the role good communication plays in romance.

_____ 2. I know how important it is to be romantic.

_____ 3. I feel comfortable having my date come to my house for dinner.

_____ 4. I know the value of creating a romantic atmosphere to go with the dinner.

_____ 5. I appreciate the importance of romantic gestures.

_____ 6. I am able to show my pleasure for caring gestures made towards me.

_____ 7. I frequently go out of my way to show my partner that I am thinking about him/her.

Scoring

70 – 60 - You are a romantic person and your partner is (or will be) lucky!

50 – 30 - You are a borderline romantic. But you seem to be making progress.

20 – 0   - You probably lack romantic skills, but it isn't that hard— you can learn!

CHAPTER 12

Backups, Returning Veterans and Instant Relationships

"I just want to keep my eyes and ears open so I don't miss a potential opportunity—
I would rather take the chance of being hurt than not do anything."

Esther

Backups, Returning Veterans and Instant Relationships are three concepts with which everyone may not be familiar, but they are real options for singles at midlife. We cannot always be in an ideal relationship, yet we need to continue to feel connected and enjoy activities with the opposite sex. In these three scenarios, both the man and the woman benefit and get something out of the relationship, although these benefits may be completely different.

Forty-seven percent of the men in our study told us they have had one or two committed relationships other than marriage. The other 53 percent told us they have had more. Forty-five percent of the women we surveyed experienced one or two committed relationships, with 55 percent confirming more. Many of these relationships for both sexes fall into one or more of our categories: Backups, Returning Veterans or Instant Relationships. The average length of the men's shortest serious relationship was 3.4 years and for the women, it was 2.5 years. Since, in the big picture of relationships, this is not a significant amount of time, the fact that more than 50 percent of both the men and the women in our study have had more than two committed relationships is understandable. Committed, of course, means different things to different people and it does not necessarily include marriage. What is also interesting is the fact that the average of the men's shortest relationships, at 3.4 years, is longer than the women's average at 2.4 years, contradicting the commonly held view that it is men who have the shortest relationships.

Backups

Essentially, we all want to find our number one true love who becomes our soulmate and that's great—but what do we do in the meantime? That is where the concept of the backup relationship comes into play. Many of us have had a relationship with a man or a woman that is uniquely personal and straightforward: You can talk about anything, you are comfortable being together and it often leads to a great sexual relationship.

But this individual is just not the right one for you in the long run— you know it and he or she knows it. When you are single at midlife or beyond, having this kind of alternative relationship, in which you both are aware the other person is not "the one" is reasonable and acceptable. You can enjoy doing things together and both still be alert to finding your soul mates.

Today, this concept is often an alternative to being alone. Finding a man or a woman with whom you have a lot in common, who can be a good friend, a travel companion and a lover, has many merits. True, he or she may not be the ultimate person for whom you are looking, but consider the benefits before you reject the concept.

Backups May Turn into the Final Act

Gloria had a Backup relationship with Mark. After a few years of several semi-serious relationships with other men, she realized Mark had always been there for her. She realized how well they knew each other and got along and how much she depended on him. He even helped her around her house with small repairs and advised her on some financial investments. Like the couple in the film *When Harry Met Sally*, it took Gloria and Mark a while before they realized they were in love. Once they did, they decided to get married. At their wedding, a huge banner was hung, which read, "Happiness is being married to your best friend."

Honesty Makes it Work

A Backup can be a transitional relationship to bridge the gap to the next permanent person in your life. These types of transitions can have great therapeutic value in that they provide a close and sharing situation, which can build confidence and help avoid the loneliness that surfaces when there is nobody in your life. The other great value of backup relationships is that you can be very honest, down to earth and comfortable. After all, there is no need for pretense or always putting your best foot forward since you don't view the person as a potential committed mate.

Backup relationships can be honest and straightforward with no deception or guile by either party. This is what, ultimately, your primary relationship should be, one in which your partner is your best friend and you can talk about everything and anything without fear of reproach or rejection. Maybe a backup relationship will give you the practice you need to actually have a sincere, close and caring relationship with a future partner.

The Dishonest Backup

The potential downside to a backup relationship is that you are the number two person…but you don't know it. Jay was dating Carol and quickly found himself truly in love with her. They went on trips, played golf, had wonderful evenings together and had a great sex life. The only problem was that Carol was unreliable and often just disappeared for weeks at a time with only the explanation that she was "busy." Of course, Jay was in a constant state of agony. Slowly he began to realize he was not the number one man in Carol's life. He began dating others, but just when he would find another interesting woman, Carol would call and invite him to an event or suggest a trip.

Still in love, Jay acquiesced. However, the roller-coaster relationship was driving him crazy. He finally realized he was simply the backup man in Carol's life. In the past, Jay frequently had backup women so he knew the signs. Nevertheless, he had a hard time facing the reality.

In this case, however, being number two just meant while Carol truly liked Jay and enjoyed his company, he was not the man she wanted to marry or have a permanent relationship with—she was in a holding pattern waiting for the number one man in her life to appear. Jay was faced with the classic backgammon stay or drop decision. After a year he finally dropped, realizing his mental health and emotional stability were at risk, because of his unrequited love for Carol.

Not for Everyone, but Possibly Rewarding

An interim backup relationship can have wonderful dividends, but only if you are emotionally able to handle one and you employ this type of relationship selectively. Although it's not for everyone, having someone who you like to be with, even if the person is not the true love you are seeking, provides company and mitigates loneliness.

Returning Veterans Are Known Quantities

Returning Veterans are similar to Backups and can also fulfill an interim role while providing more positives since you already know the person from a past encounter. Consider the advantages of returning to date a past love. This presumes, of course, that you left the past relationship with no hard feelings or bitterness and that returning to some sort of dating scenario is acceptable to both parties. There are many advantages—you obviously know the person, you probably still like one another and, presumably, you have some things in common. And guess what? It's possible the man or woman with whom you play this interim role may be the one you actually end up with!

It Only Works if You Don't Burn Bridges

Clyde, at fifty, has dated many women who were Returning Veterans. He successfully practiced positive Casanova-like behavior during his youth: never lie, stay friends, be gentlemanly and don't say negative things about any woman. He didn't burn his bridges. At this point, Clyde didn't want a serious relationship, but found great friendship and companionship with former flames. Many women and men who left earlier relationships have discovered they still have much in common five, ten, twenty or thirty years later and resume dating.

Sometimes Returning Veterans become permanent relationships, possibly ending up in marriage, but even if they don't, this type of relationship represents a sort of oasis in the desert which rewards each party with a sense of stability and mental rebalancing while they contemplate their next move in life. Probably you, like so many others, know someone who in later life reconnected with a man or woman from the past and found wonderful happiness? This miraculous reconnection often happens during a high school or college reunion.

So don't overlook the Returning Veteran as an option when you reenter the dating game. Initiating a call to someone who was once in your life may potentially lead to a very interesting and promising connection. Don't be shy about making the call. This is another case of "What do you have to lose?" At the least, you will reconnect and say hello to someone who once was and may still be important to you. The fact that a statistically measurable percentage of women in our survey felt class reunions were good places to meet people means they essentially endorsed the Returning Veteran philosophy.

The Returning Veteran Can Be Everlasting

Sometimes, the Returning Veteran turns out to be the real love of your life. Netta, a fifty-year-old New Yorker received a call from her high school boyfriend, Keith, who lived in New Mexico. As they talked, they found they still had much in common and began a long distance relationship. Due to the wonderful low-cost travel and communication networks that now exist, reconnecting was easy. Within two years they decided it was time to make their relationship permanent and she moved to Santa Fe where they were married.

In a similar case, actress Carol Channing, at the age of eighty-two, married her junior high school boyfriend, Harry, after a seventy-year separation. Harry called Carol after a friend told him she had fondly written of him in her autobiography and was now single. The wedding invitation featured a reproduction of a picture of the two of them together in junior high. Now that's a true Returning Veteran. Harry's friend commented, "It's a thrilling and life-enforcing thing you have decided to do."

When former New York City Mayor Rudolph Guliani publicly announced he was divorcing his wife of sixteen years, television personality Donna Hanover, so that he could be with another woman, the story appeared in newspapers around the country. At a time of great distress and upset in Hanover's life, an old high school sweetheart of hers, who lived across the continent in California, took the time to track down her phone number, call her and gently inquire if she were planning to attend their school reunion. And guess what? They met, fell in love all over again and recently married. Perhaps if you make a call to a past love, you too will find your soul mate.

The Instant Relationship: An Exciting Option

The third alternative is the "here and now" philosophy of the Instant Relationship. Contrary to what you may have been conditioned to believe all of your life, moving quickly into a new relationship may yield wonderful results. At the least, it is another option. Having reached maturity and, hopefully, being wiser, you now know what you want and don't want in a partner so you can immediately, or almost immediately, ascertain if a person is right for you. At this time in your life, it no longer takes weeks or months to determine a person's good (or bad) qualities. Age and experience once again work to your advantage.

This alternative is not for the conservative individual, but for those who have confidence both in themselves and in their own intuition about other people. In the words of the human potential guru Ram Dass, popularized by Werner Erhard in his EST awareness training seminars of the 1970s and 1980s, a "be here now" attitude about yourself is necessary to enable this sort of instant, life-changing decision.

This is not a call to arms to run out and get into a relationship or get married in the first weeks or months of meeting a desirable man or woman, but we should all be in a position by now to make relatively quick decisions about the opposite sex. We know if there is physical chemistry—that certainly doesn't take very long to determine. Compatibility or emotional chemistry is next and that clearly takes more time, but you should have a pretty good indication early on if you are on the same wavelength. And certainly initial chemistry can vaporize very fast if the person turns out to have one or more incompatible traits.

Who Says You Can't Do It?

Let's say you have just met a seemingly special person and you say to yourself, "Gee, I can't get involved here. I just got out of a relationship—this would be an instant rebound. All my friends and my analyst have told me not to do that." Well, the truth is, at midlife, time is of the essence.

Although subscribing to the "living in the moment" theory may not be for everyone, it can certainly make your life much more rewarding and fulfilling. This is in direct contrast to the often-prevailing theory that you shouldn't get immediately involved with someone who has just gotten out of a relationship. This theory says the person has not healed, is just interested in forgetting his or her past and the situation will simply end with both parties getting hurt. Sure that is possible, but it's just as possible they are both meant for one another and theirs will be a solid relationship.

If you are one of the cautious people who shy away from someone who has just ended a relationship because you fear you will just be a rebound, consider the fact that it is possible you are the right one for this person. So don't be cowardly, give the person the benefit of the doubt and give yourself a break. If you invest enough time, you will find out if you and the person you just met are compatible and are ready to take the relationship to the next level.

Sometimes Instant Relationships Are Just Transitional

Instant Relationships do not always work, of course. Sylvia, a woman in our study, tells us she met Rudy, who she thought was the love of her life. Three months prior to their meeting, his wife of thirty years had died after a lengthy bout with cancer. Sylvia was the first woman Rudy had gone out with. He was lonely and afraid of his own mortality. They quickly fell into an intimate relationship. For the first six months, Sylvia was there to comfort him in his grief and often wipe his tears. A year passed and as Rudy healed, they both realized that although they cared about each other, they had little in common. Their relationship had been built around his sadness and her ability to nurture him. They amicably parted and whenever he sees Sylvia, Rudy tells her, "You saved my life and made me want to live again."

You Never Know Unless You Try

Joyce, a forty-eight-year-old widow from the Midwest, had an initial date with Hal, who she found extremely interesting and with whom she felt instant chemistry. During the course of the date she discovered he had left a three-year relationship only three weeks earlier. Her immediate reaction was, *I can't trust this man. How will I know if he really wants me or is just using me to forget his former girlfriend?* She elected to reject him rather than take the chance. Six months later, a friend described a terrific man she had met and with whom she was having a wonderful relationship. You guessed it! The man was Hal (it turned out she had met him the week after Joyce had rejected him). She told Joyce, "He is one of the most open and caring men I have met in a long time. I feel this is going to be the one." He was and they were married before the year was out.

Joyce was left wondering about her judgment. Should she have taken the chance with Hal? She will obviously never know, but the lesson may well be, don't over think every situation to the extent that you end up depriving yourself of what may be a wonderful experience and a great future.

Just When Is Later to You?

Mason's attitude on living in the here and now is somewhat conditioned by several experiences from his past. He believes it is part of the reason he would quickly make a connection with a woman if it was warranted and the proper chemistry was there. He suffered through the 1989 San Francisco earthquake as well as being at the site of the World Trade Center bombing in 1993. Having lived through such traumatic events, he realizes life is not infinite and he tends to live in the here and now.

Mason feels once you have something happen in your life that brings that sort of reality to the forefront, you begin to plan with a little more urgency. You realize that later may be too late. We hope you gain from this book the realization that time is precious. At midlife and beyond, you should stop waiting around for a man or a woman to somehow appear in your life. Be proactive and act in positive ways to reach out and find love.

Even taking a risk that may lead to being hurt is worth it. At least this way you will have many wonderful moments. As Esther told us, "My husband died a year go and I don't want to wait until I am seventy to find another great relationship. So, even though I know the person I am with now is probably not 'the one,' he keeps me from being lonely and makes me happy. I will keep my eyes open so I don't miss a potential opportunity for my true love to appear. And I am willing to take the chance of being hurt rather than not do anything."

Quiz – Chapter 12

Are you ready to experience a relationship that may be less than permanent or perfect? This quick quiz will help you evaluate if you can accept a relationship that is less than ideal. Please rate yourself:

10 points for a "yes"; 5 points for an "undecided"; 0 points for a "no"

Ranking	Question
_____	1. I am open to the possibility of a Backup relationship.
_____	2. I am open to the possibility of a Returning Veteran relationship.
_____	3. I am open to the possibility of an Instant Relationship.
_____	4. I have previously been in one of these types of relationship and I would do it again.
_____	5. A friend is now in one of these types of relationship and I support this person.
_____	6. I would rather be in an interim relationship than not in a relationship at all.
_____	7. I recognize that time is of the essence and waiting for later is a poor option.

Scoring

70 – 60 - Your eyes are definitely open to all possibilities.

50 – 30 - You are becoming more broadminded and seem ready for this kind of relationship.

20 – 0 - Do what you are comfortable with and don't push it if you feel one of these relationships is not for you.

CHAPTER 13

The Sex Part:
Do We Still Want It?

"I didn't know sex could be so wonderful!"
Marie

W hen you have someone who loves you and would do anything in the
world for you and you feel the same, it can be the most wonderful
feeling in the world. Human beings were designed for love and a healthy sex
life, but really rewarding sex requires the ultimate trust, vulnerability, honesty and total emotional commitment.

The need for love, intimacy and sex is one of the strongest drives we
experience. According to famed psychiatrist Abraham Maslow, it is third
only to our need for food and shelter. And the men and women in our study
of midlife singles told us they spent a lot of time thinking about sex. Many
fantasized about sex with different partners, in different positions and in
exotic locations. Why all the preoccupation with sex even as one reaches
middle age and beyond? As one of our study respondents wrote, "Because it
still feels good and I really enjoy it."

Sex: The Glue That Ultimately Bonds Us

We have all pondered how we can be so sexually attracted to one person and
not another. Sexual attraction is very mysterious and when chemistry happens,
both people know it instantly. At that moment, the other person seems differ-

ent from any other you have ever met. During that first encounter, two people can often feel they want to have sex and may even instantly decide they want to be intimate. And some may even think they want to spend their lives together...their pulses quicken and they experience heightened senses of awareness (the soulmate concept described in the final chapter of this book). They instinctively know they would have a passionate, fulfilling life together.

As mentioned previously, 56 percent of the men and 33 percent of the women in our study are currently involved in relationships. When we asked the men to describe their current relationships, they said their partners were:

sexy and sizzling	(35%)
compatible and comfortable	(26%)
funny	(15%)
supportive of me	(11%)
trusting	(8%)
stimulating	(5%)

New Relationships

Eric said, "Even though I have been married once and in several relationships, this one seems so new to me." It is noteworthy that men describing their partners as "sexy and sizzling" were in the majority (35 percent), even though men did not select this in our survey as the number one quality they were looking for. "Compatible and comfortable," the number two description, supports our contention that most men do not want what they consider high maintenance or taxing women.

The women described their partners in their current relationships as:

committed to me	(33%)
equal partner	(25%)
common values	(14%)
shared activities	(14%)
integrity	(8%)
spiritual	(6%)

We noted that the qualities both men and women previously said they were ideally looking for were somewhat different than what they actually found! As frequently happens in relationships, we end up with real people who are different than our fantasy mates. Remember the point we learned earlier, that one shouldn't reject people based on what they initially say? What people say they want and what they really want or are willing to settle for may be quite different from the reality. It is also worthy to note that none of the descriptions of the qualities both men and women found appealing in the other overlapped.

The Excitement Remains

Since romance and sex play such a major role in fulfilling relationships, we were glad to find most people have basically worked through many of the early mysteries and myths that often surrounded sex in our youth. And while some things may be forgotten, almost everyone remembers the first time they had sex. Most are now able to put that event in perspective and recognize what sexual compatibility (or lack of it) means today. Hopefully, mature couples will realistically deal with sex in a manner that makes them both comfortable. If sex is not a part of a relationship, many mature couples are also able to deal with that on a realistic basis.

The Answers Are Still Not Totally Apparent

In midlife, some people are frustrated and wonder how they can bring back their earlier passion for sex. Conversely, if they haven't had great sex lives, they ask, "Can I or will I ever have one?" And then there are those who don't know they have had poor sex lives because they haven't had enough experience to know the difference (the good news for these people is that they aren't in despair about missing it). As we age, men and women can suffer from age- or disease-related sexual dysfunctions, lack of desire, inability to achieve orgasm or male impotence, all of which may interfere with rewarding sex lives. These things may also play a role in our mental desire or libido. Women and men change physically as they grow older and may not feel that they look sexy. This in turn may make them not feel sexy.

One man in our study told us, "I look good in a suit, but now I have a beer belly and am no longer the muscular college athlete I once was. It makes me think twice before wanting to undress in front of a woman."

Religion can also play a big role in the way many people view sex. Some religious denominations frown on sex outside of marriage. Many men and women (although more women) who are over fifty got married as virgins more than thirty years ago. Both partners often valued this and, in those days, parents frequently put a high value on their daughters remaining virgins until married. After twenty, thirty or more years of marriage, some women (and a few men) who are now divorced or widowed, wonder, *Should I remain chaste until I marry again? And what if I never remarry—do I forgo sex forever?*

Obviously, our society is much more liberal now. While some people still have strong convictions that they should wait for marriage to have sexual relations, and they do, many are now feeling it is okay to be intimate as long as they are in a committed relationship. Still others opt to have sex after a few dates or maybe even after one date. This is a personal decision and one on which we have chosen not to give advice—it is your decision alone.

For Many, Sex Has Come Full Circle

Adam, a man in our study who is now in his early fifties, married Sophia when he was in his early twenties. They were divorced after a lengthy marriage and Adam has been single for two years. He was one of the men who married early because, by his own admission, "I dated Sophia for two years and she still wouldn't have sex with me unless I married her."

Of course, during his marriage, Adam heard many stories from his single male friends about the new sexual revolution and all of the women that were willing to have casual sex. However, now, as he begins his single life and is dating, he is hearing a similar story to the one he heard in his youth. "I won't have sex until you are committed to me." His lament, "I can't believe it! It seems as though all of these women have come full circle and have become almost celibate again. I missed everything!"

The Question of Infidelity

The men and women we interviewed stressed fidelity as perhaps the most important bond in lasting relationships. Few situations can wreak greater emotional havoc than *not* remaining monogamous. Our respondents all stated that once the trust in a relationship has been broken, love is usually lost.

While some of our respondents did forgive their partners, it was very difficult for most to continue the relationship as before. While one partner's affair did not ruin every relationship, men and women both said it was nearly impossible to regain their former levels of confidence. Although some tried to weather the storm, the vast majority reported they eventually broke up with their partners as a result of the infidelity.

There are, we feel, important points for women and men in this scenario. The vast majority of men who have an affair outside of marriage or a committed relationship do so for the excitement of having sex with someone new. It does not necessarily mean they have, in fact, fallen in love with the other women or that their partners have not met their sexual needs. However, many of the women whose partners were unfaithful asked themselves, "What did I do that didn't meet his needs?" The answer is probably nothing; often men have affairs to raise their self-esteem and because sex is available. So, although you may want to end the relationship, it is important you not lose confidence in yourself over a partner's infidelity.

Most women who have affairs state that their infidelities normally involve love as well as sex. Men can usually walk away from an affair; women frequently grieve. Recently, we have seen this in political and social circles when Kerry Kennedy, forty-three, daughter of the late Senator Robert Kennedy and niece of the late President John F. Kennedy, split from her husband of thirteen years, Andrew Cuomo, son of former New York Governor Mario Cuomo, after her affair with a married man who chose to stay with his wife was exposed. This is why infidelity by a woman can be a greater threat to the relationship—the woman is often deeply involved. Our study respondents told us they thought it much harder for many men to forgive women who have strayed than for many women to forgive unfaithful men.

When we asked our participants if they thought either partner should confess an affair once it is over, both men and women overwhelmingly said "No." One said, "Confession tends to make the injured party feel depressed and a feeling of having been betrayed takes over and rules his or her emotions. Trust is so important to the relationship, that once it is gone, it is almost impossible to regain."

High Tech Sex: Yes, It Exists. But Why?

Some people related to us they have had the experience of high tech sex on the Internet, which is seen by some partners as a form of infidelity. They told us they are very open about their desires, discuss how they experience the act of sex and what they want and enjoy. Jenny, a woman in our study, told us while she is in a relationship, she can sometimes talk more frankly on the Internet with her high tech partner, who she does not plan to meet, than she can with her real partner with whom she is intimate. This illustrates how poorly many couples communicate. It shows an underlying lack of commitment to the current relationship. Why should someone with a loving partner be talking sex with others on the Internet?

Be that as it may, instead of having an anonymous Internet discussion, why not begin a dialogue with your partner? Try it. You may be surprised how responsive he or she will be to your candor (unless of course, you really know your partner will be offended, in which case, consider moving on—you are definitely not communicating, in more ways than one).

If you have these types of contact on the Internet, even though there is no physical touching, it will be perceived by many as a form of infidelity. Most men and women are not comfortable when their partners engage in this type of activity. The trust disappears and it is difficult, if not downright impossible, to get the relationship back on the same course.

Problems Don't Disappear with Age

Two couples in our survey told us of their sexual challenges. At this point in time, they had not found solutions for their problems. The first couple is Ted and Claudia. Ted said Claudia has a real phobia about taking her clothes off in front of him and has always been this way. Even though they have been sleeping together for six months, she still takes her clothes off in the bathroom and slips into bed wearing her robe. Only after the lights are out will she let him take her robe off. While Ted said it sometimes was very arousing to remove her robe, he would prefer she felt comfortable undressing in front of him.

The second couple who spoke to us about their sexual issues, Michelle and Harvey, had a different problem. Michelle told us Harvey loves to prolong the final peak of his climax for as long as possible. She said, "It sometimes takes too long for him to be satisfied." She told us after about thirty minutes of intense lovemaking she was spent, and then for the next hour, her mind was elsewhere—making grocery lists, planning the next day and thinking of other things. Harvey never seemed to notice her mind had strayed during this period.

Both couples professed they loved each other, clicked in other areas of their life and want to make sex for their partner more rewarding. There are many ways to accomplish this. Having a frank discussion is certainly the first, logical option, but if this is still not comfortable for one or both of the partners, counseling with a sex therapist is another option. However, this requires that both partners acknowledge their problem with openness and have a willingness to work it out.

Books and magazines also can provide advice on sexual techniques. One of the classics is *The Joy of Sex*. It has outstanding, very tasteful illustrations. Sometimes women have a harder time achieving orgasm than men and, if this is the case for you, you will find especially helpful techniques in this book.

If you are one of the women or men who haven't yet experienced great sex, there is a whole new level of sexual information available that wasn't around decades ago. Perhaps when you were young you did not have a lot of sexual experience or knowledge about sexual satisfaction, nor did your partner. If sex has never been interesting or fulfilling and you wish it could be, don't be embarrassed about seeking help and finding good counseling. Mature physical love between two willing, enthusiastic partners can bring wonderful satisfaction.

Marie's Story: One Woman's Evolution

Marie told us, "In discussing dating, women need a thorough understanding of the importance and relevance of sex to a relationship." Marie described her own evolution from a woman with two children who had a problematic marriage for thirty years to a liberated single woman.

We heard over and over again from other women in our study the theme she expressed. Recognizing that her story could have significance for many women, we asked her to describe her situation. Marie is a resident of Cleveland, a business executive in the computer software industry, a former owner-operator of two businesses; she was raised a Catholic, has appeared in a business magazine as a role model for newly single women over forty, is active in social and civic projects in Cleveland and has a graduate degree.

Marie said, "For many women, sexual intimacy is a major determinate for knowing if you have found the right man, your soul mate, if you will. Sexual intimacy and satisfaction are big parts of the ideal relationship. If you believe sexual intimacy is important to your overall relationship, how can you make a determination that he is the right man if you have not experienced satisfying sex with him?

"That was my dilemma when I got divorced. I sat in the kitchen of a friend's house bemoaning my fate of enforced celibacy. I felt I could never take my clothes off in front of someone who wasn't my husband—I would be too shy. I was sure I could never have sex with someone unless I was positive he loved me! I told my friend I probably would miss sex as much as any part of my marriage. At that time, I really thought I knew what good sex was like.

"Alas, I was from the generation raised to believe sex was only proper in marriage. I had gone from college and virginity to marriage. The first and only sexual experiences I had for thirty-plus years were with my husband and it seemed to be good. It never occurred to me then that I would ever have to make a decision about having sex with another man. After the divorce, I was terrified of dating, as I heard every guy expected sex at the end of every evening and I knew I just could not do that!

"Fast-forward three months; at that point, out of sheer desperation, misery and boredom I courageously took the plunge and went to a singles event. After a period of time with no one approaching me, I realized I might have to initiate a conversation, so I picked out the best looking guy, walked up to him and hesitantly said, 'Hi, I'm Marie.' Fortunately, he responded intelligently, 'Hi, I'm Gene,' and we began talking. The luck of the Irish was with me that day, because Gene was a very great guy.

"We began to date and we had great times. We talked and laughed and candidly discussed our past lives. The result of this, however, was that the sexual attraction was becoming increasingly more powerful. I knew he was feeling the same thing, but he did not make any overt moves or attempt to push me into something he didn't think I was ready for. Slowly I changed my attitude about sex and to make a long and lovely story short, it happened naturally and beautifully after our eighth date. What a surprise! I certainly didn't know sex could be so wonderful!

"My relationship with Gene was full of marvelous intimacy and enhanced my desire to continue on to the next step of the relationship. It was the most positive and healthy experience of my newly single life and it opened my eyes to what superb sex really was. Today, I look back with real fondness on the years Gene and I shared, because if I had not changed my mind and decided to make sex a part of the relationship, I would not have realized there is great satisfaction and fulfillment in the kind of friendship and connection I had with this man.

"Although the relationship was not permanent, he brought new meaning and happiness to my life, which had been made to seem almost insignificant because of the bad treatment I had received from my former husband. I was on the verge of becoming a bitter lady, frozen and turned off forever. I felt all men were louses. All of these negative results could easily have continued if this second man in my life hadn't made the sexual intimacy part of our relationship meaningful."

If you are a man or woman who has not had a fulfilling sex life, now is the time for you to learn how to make this important area of intimacy satisfying. Your changing attitudes and the life experience you have gathered can help you enjoy this part of a new relationship and experience sex in an entirely new light.

Therapists?

There are many psychotherapists who treat sexually dysfunctional individuals. If you are a woman or man who has been told you are inadequate and you suspect it may have been your partner, there is a good chance you are right. Visiting a psychotherapist trained in sexual dysfunction may help you solve the problem.

Katie, a woman in our study, recently began dating Stan, a handsome, amusing, East Coast distributor for several Italian designers. Katie is a buyer for a successful New York boutique. Stan and Katie shared many common interests, including the fact they both were single parents of teenaged children. Their relationship progressed to the point that Stan told Katie that when his wife left him and their children, she proceeded to "go sexually crazy," finding new men at every turn.

Several dates later, Katie and Stan had sex. After several attempts, Katie discovered sex with Stan generally took less than two minutes with minimal foreplay. When she initiated a conversation with him regarding their unsatisfactory sex life, Stan suggested she "did not stimulate him enough." Katie wondered if she could she have stimulated him to the point at which he could have changed his behavior. Finally, she talked to a therapist and understood the fault was not hers. Stan was simply ignorant when it came to sex.

Always remember there are two sides to every relationship and you are only hearing one side of the story. The worst part of this story is that Stan tried to make Katie believe it was her fault! A partner who blames you for bad sex is highly suspect.

If one is to be a good partner, one needs to have a certain sexual knowledge as well as sensitivity. You need to be aware of your own individual sexuality: what arouses you, what you prefer and what presents obstacles. We all need to be in touch with our desires and emotional conflicts. Once we are aware of our body and our needs, we can find the way to a healthier and more joyous sex life. The all-important next step is that you be able to communicate with your partner in a forthright and sensitive manner about this sensitive topic.

There Are Two Sides to Every (Sex) Story

One of the more recent episodes in Chuck's life relates to a woman, Natasha, who he had dated on and off for fifteen years. She had recently broken up with Steve, a man with whom she had lived for ten years. Chuck started dating her again (a Returning Veteran!). By a twist of fate, Chuck was on a plane with Walter, a mutual friend of both Natasha and Steve. In the course of the conversation, Chuck and Walter began discussing why Natasha and Steve had broken up. Walter commented that, in fact, Steve had said Natasha was not "very sexually interesting."

Since Chuck had a sexual relationship with Natasha for many years (a fact Walter was not aware of), he was shocked and blurted out, "Boy, is Steve clueless! Natasha is one of the most sexual women I have ever known." Walter, of course, was astounded—first, by the fact Chuck possessed such knowledge of Natasha, and second, that she was, indeed, highly sexual.

Now, of course, Chuck committed a rookie error: He inadvertently betrayed a confidence with Natasha! So, of course, as soon as the plane landed, Chuck immediately called Natasha and told her what he had said to Walter. Chuck wasn't sure whether she would be angry or accepting of his revelations, but he knew he needed to tell her.

Natasha chuckled and said, "Steve didn't have a clue about sex, but I stayed with him because I loved everything else about him."

The moral to this story? If your partner ever tells you that you are not sexually pleasing or that it's your fault, just assume he or she is the one who doesn't get it. It's more than likely your partner's problem not yours.

Some Men Really Have No Clue

Amy was having a discussion with her good friend Arthur about her dating experience with Eugene, a man she had met three weeks earlier at a charity event. She told Arthur that Eugene was a really interesting man, but when she kissed him, the experience wasn't a good one. At that time, Eugene had been dating actively for more than five years after many years of marriage. Amy felt kissing was important for her since she valued physical contact. Arthur, being a relatively experienced man, explained this was probably only the tip of the iceberg, so to speak, and Eugene was also likely to be very bad as a sexual partner due to his lack of experience. Amy's comment was, "But hasn't he learned anything during the time he has been dating? Why would any woman even date a man who is so inept at kissing—much less sleep with him?"

Arthur explained that unless one of the other women who Eugene dated had taken the time to tell him how poorly he performed, it was likely Eugene has simply remained in the dark about his lack of skill.

One week later, Amy called Arthur and said, "You were absolutely right. I had sex with Eugene and he was just awful! He was totally inattentive to me on all levels; it just seemed like he was a beginner and I was his first sexual encounter. I am sure he had a good time, but if that is his level of sensitivity, he isn't going to date me again. If all men were like that I would give up sex forever."

Arthur explained that the greatest favor Amy could do for Eugene was to tell him about his problem. Unfortunately, Amy's attitude was, "I am not running a training program and if a man his age hasn't learned anything about women, I don't want to be the one to teach him, and anyway, at his amateur level, it's conceivable he is beyond help. It's 'Goodbye Eugene.' I am simply going to say, 'I don't think we are compatible and I just don't feel there is any chemistry between us.'"

Some Men Need (Sexual) Help

If you are a man who seems to have an unusually high rate of rejection, particularly just after you have had sex with a woman, maybe you need to think about this as a potential problem. Casanova was much more concerned with a woman's sexual pleasure than his own. He proved that attentiveness to a woman's needs works.

A man who spends two minutes quickly having an orgasm, then rolls over and falls asleep is not high on most women's list of desirable males. Most women feel sex is not just sex and there must be feeling on the part of the man—in short, romantic sex. Kissing, touching and general affection before and after sex are important components of the sexual process. Most women welcome extended foreplay by the man before sex. Women need to be aroused and like to feel they are appreciated. Mature men need to remember that the women they are with may have had bad experiences sexually and emotionally.

Men who pay attention to women's needs, make the body/mind connection and know how to display intimacy and true affection will always be prized. Women who are not sexually responsive are not the norm. If a man treats a woman well and if he is physically attentive and sexually romantic, the woman will respond. Men who blame women for their sexual inadequacies had better get some help. Women who have been through this in their pasts are far less willing to accept such behavior—they've gotten smarter.

No matter what our age, sex is an integral part of a relationship and communication is an integral part of sex. It should not be an afterthought; it is intimately connected to all parts of our lives, from our self-esteem to our physical health to the strength of our relationships with others. We never grow too old for love and intimacy. Understanding our partners' likes and dislikes and developing intimate communication is crucial. So talk! And love.

Quiz – Chapter 13

Sex is an integral part of a relationship— we never grow too old for sex and romance. This quick quiz will help you evaluate your sexual intimacy quotient. Please rate yourself:

10 points for a "yes"; 5 points for an "undecided"; 0 points for a "no"

Ranking	Question
_____	1. I have experienced great sex.
_____	2. I think sex is important and I want it in my life.
_____	3. For me, sex in midlife is as exciting as it was when I was younger.
	4. I take time to be a caring and sensitive lover.
_____	5. I understand how important fidelity is to most people.
_____	6. I do not need to go outside a satisfying relationship for sexual stimulation.
_____	7. If requested by my partner, I would go for sexual counseling.

Scoring

70 – 60 - You are definitely a sexual person and prepared for a romantic relationship.

50 – 30 - Sounds like you're close to being there and are considering the options.

20 – 0 - Sex may not be important to you in a relationship–if this is the case be sure your partner understands your feeling.

CHAPTER 14

Dating the Powerful, the Famous or the Very Rich

"If you have the opportunity to date a powerful or famous man, it will be exhilarating and fun, but just keep in mind what it is—fun."

Gayle

For most of us, opportunities to date powerful, well known or rich individuals were not generally available in our youth. In later life, however, there may be ample opportunities to meet powerful, well known or extremely wealthy people of the opposite sex. While this discussion covers the reaction of both men and women, it mostly focuses on women reacting to men.

The favorable reactions by women to men who fall into these categories have always been viewed with envy, awe or often disdain by ordinary men who themselves do not possess the same advantages.

If Men Are Envious of Anything, This Is It

A man with powerful connections and influence often has the most magnetic of the qualities we discuss in this chapter, since power, be it fiscal, political, or fame, represents the epitome of strength to which women are drawn. Clearly, attraction to power has everything to do with presence and little to do with physical appearance.

Powerful Men Are Used to Being In Control

Jennifer, a woman in our study, told us about dating a United States senator, one of the ultimate power positions. Some of her favorite stories center on his being able to get last minute reservations and frequently the best seat in the house at sold out theaters or restaurants as well as the VIP treatment when they traveled.

However, after a while, Jennifer got tired of his being recognized everywhere they went, tired of strangers coming up to talk and tired of all the autograph seekers. The senator seemed to enjoy all of this. The attention made him come alive. But when they were alone, it was as if his charming façade dropped. He became reticent, said little and was becoming boring. After a year, she opted out of the relationship, but will never forget this time of total glamour. She highly recommends a power relationship for anyone seeking a period of excitement, but says, "Don't get too attached. He may soon be gone!"

Men Are Intimidated by Fame, Women Are Drawn to It

Fame is a close second draw to power since many women also find famous men to be exciting. Some women are interested in meeting well-known men even if they are married! Becky, who dated a very famous man (who was incidentally, short, overweight and balding), described how women would approach him and flirt, even when she was standing right next to him.

Sammy Davis Jr. wrote one of the great descriptions of the appeal of fame in his autobiography. He said, "I am black, Jewish, I have one eye, I am short and I am ugly, but I can get any woman in the room by just snapping my fingers—isn't that amazing?" It certainly is. Power, fame and wealth are three great aphrodisiacs.

Should you find yourself with the option of dating a powerful or famous person, just remember these men are used to having a lot of women literally throw themselves at them. They are used to having their own way—often by snapping their fingers. Sammy Davis was not the exception, he was the rule. As Nick Nolte, the actor, said, "I just wanted to be famous so I could get laid."

If you have an opportunity to have a date with a famous or powerful man it will be exhilarating and fun, but just keep in mind what it is—fun. The odds of creating a long-term relationship with one of these men are low, so try not to get emotionally involved and just enjoy the moment.

Elizabeth, a fifty-three-year-old divorcee in our study, once dated a man with an international reputation in the technology field. He had over twenty patents and had written numerous books and articles. He was frequently invited to lecture and received awards worldwide. She soon realized this was his life; his work was his mistress. He was so obsessive he would scribble notes on restaurant napkins, during flights and even carried a pencil light for writing during operas! Elizabeth loved being part of the adoration that followed him everywhere. But after he went on a trip to Paris and returned with a beautiful countess, he never called her again. Six months later, she learned he had dropped the countess and was pursuing a well-known socialite from Boston. Luckily, Elizabeth was a secure woman and took the relationship for what it was—a wonderful dalliance that gave her an insider's view of fame.

Some Men May Find It Exciting, Too

Famous and powerful women, like movie stars, political and business personalities, even queens and princesses, seem to have more difficulty finding companions than their male counterparts. Most powerful women tend to stay within their own social structure, reducing the possibility of meeting an "ordinary" man. When so-called power couples do get together, it can lead to fulfillment or, very often, friction. In other circumstances, when powerful or famous women have relationships with ordinary men, such relationships flower or wither, depending on whether or not the man possesses good self-esteem. Should the occasion arise, men should view dating famous or powerful women as simply another relationship opportunity.

Wealth Doesn't Mean Better

In the third category, wealthy men and women often are interested in forming a long-lasting relationship. In fact, you may not even know he or she has money until you have dated the person for a period of time. Often the wealthy dress very casually, don't pay excessive attention to their looks and do not drive luxury cars. They appear to be just like any other person. This is also why dating the rich does not bring the same level of excitement as dating the powerful or famous. Rich men and women can be very boring and unexciting—just like poor ones.

Although far more men than women fall in this category, money seems to be the one attribute that has the least draw for midlife women, according to our survey.

A relationship with someone who is wealthy is certainly a realistic possibility. While some of the wealthy are hard to spot, others are easier, because they broadcast their success. Some women have dated men who say, "I don't want a woman to want me for my money!" Yet they spend the greater part of the first date telling the woman about their great business success and how much money they have accumulated.

Many men find themselves rejected for their excessive boorishness. But if a woman decides he's got enough other redeeming qualities to be a "keeper" and he is very wealthy, she should be aware that generally, these men are used to having people acquiesce to them in business and are often highly competitive. This tends to make them controlling and demanding in their personal lives—a personality trait many women have learned the hard way to avoid.

Some Women Have Acquired Wealth

On the flip side, today a lot of women also have money and the situation is reversed. Divorce, inheritance or very successful careers have made many mature women financially independent, so they now have to think about protecting their wealth from male predators who see dollar signs. Wealthy women frequently buy designer clothes, expensive jewelry and upscale cars. They are therefore more easily identified. Conversely, while it's true many wealthy men also exhibit these same tendencies, a percentage of them maintain a low profile and their wealth is not visible.

It's interesting that many women with money are exactly the opposite of many men, who tend to talk about their success and money on the first date. Women rarely, if ever, bring up the subject. Most women are very circumspect about discussing their financial positions.

A "Buyer Beware" Situation for Women: Treasure Hunters Are Pros!

Unfortunately for women, men who are on the "hunt" often cultivate romantic, caring and charming qualities and are, therefore, very hard to spot. They seem to do everything right. It behooves a woman with significant financial assets to be on guard

Madeleine, who has a substantial net worth of her own, was dating a man she felt was sincere and in love with her. He gave her a diamond ring, not as an engagement ring but as a present and symbol of their relationship, "to show his great devotion" to her. She naturally was excited this man was so generous and thoughtful and she clearly felt he was her financial equal (which, in this case, was his plan). Unfortunately he made a fatal error. The ring didn't fit her finger so she took it to a jeweler to get it sized.

The jeweler called her back the next day and said, "Come and get this piece of glass, I don't work on fake jewelry." She got lucky. Even if it isn't "romantic," women with money will find it in their own best interests to fully understand the financial history of any man they intend to marry. You need to ask the hard questions, no man who is truly in love with you will resent your queries.

Just as All Women Are Not Gold Diggers, Neither Are All Men

In the reverse situation, Clare, the chief financial officer of a major corporation, was the high-income partner. With an MBA from an Ivy League school and a Ph.D. in Finance, her salary and her intellectual qualities were top notch. Finally she found a perfect relationship. She met a man who was very proud of her accomplishments and not in the least threatened by them. He was a business manager for a non-profit foundation. He was very secure and he felt his work was making a difference in the world. While not "in her league" financially, he was not threatened by her success, was happy with his own status and was not interested in her money.

Relationships with Fame and Power Are Not Realistic: Money Is

Dating the very wealthy is no longer a remote possibility—it is a very real scenario for many mature people. While in principle, money shouldn't matter, it usually does. If one of you has it and the other doesn't, it can be important to either party. It isn't a disaster, but it is a new variable that will need your attention. If you are lucky enough to have any of these three types of people come into your life: the famous, the powerful or the wealthy, do not prejudge the individual. Take the risk. If the relationship doesn't last, it will be an exciting time in your life, and if it does, you have found your soul mate.

Quiz – Chapter 14

In midlife, you may have opportunities to date the powerful, the famous or the very rich. This quick quiz will help you evaluate if this is what you really want. Please rate yourself:

10 points for a "yes"; 5 points for an "undecided"; 0 points for a "no"

Ranking   **Question**

_____ 1. If given a chance, I would enjoy dating a powerful person.

_____ 2. If given a chance, I would enjoy dating a famous person.

_____ 3. If given a chance, I would enjoy dating a very rich person.

_____ 4. In any case, I would remain "grounded" and enjoy the experience.

_____ 5. "Gold diggers" are fairly easy for me to spot.

_____ 6. I would not be intimidated by a powerful, famous or wealthy person.

_____ 7. I am realistic and know my chances of finding true love among the famous and powerful are slim, but I will accept the relationship for what it is.

Scoring

70 – 60 - You would enjoy one or more of these opportunities.

50 – 30 - You are realistic, but you are not sure you would enjoy life in the fast lane.

20 – 0 - You are secure in knowing these experiences are not for everyone and your choice is for a more "normal" relationship.

CHAPTER 15

Why Would Someone Want Me?

"In midlife, you need to clearly determine your 'must have' and 'can't deal with' qualities sooner rather than later."

Barry

There are advantages to being mature and experienced. As we age most of us arrive at a much clearer understanding of ourselves. We are who we are. In other words, as the Velveteen Rabbit said, "We are real." In midlife, we have a realistic understanding of our good qualities (and, hopefully, our bad), what we have to offer and why others might want us.

The Opposite Sex May Still Remain a Mystery

Many argue we are basically "formed" when we reach twenty, but even if this is true, there is still a lot of refining of ourselves that occurs as we age. Major adjustments that continue not only into our middle years, but beyond include problem solving, crisis resolution, acquired knowledge, grieving experiences and resolution, failure and success management, and nurturing skills to name just a few of the key developmental areas that mold our lives. While our basic values may stay the same, there is little similarity between who we are at twenty and who we become in later life.

Once we figure *ourselves* out, we can then turn to analyzing the *opposite sex*. However, there are often characteristics about the opposite sex we *still* don't understand despite our maturity and past experiences. This knowledge gap exists because we have never consciously taken the time and effort to learn.

Our survey revealed much information on the relative strengths and weaknesses of individuals and it pinpointed the traits that respondents believe caused their marriages and relationships to fail. These basic flaws were not easily detected during early courtships and marriages, but over time they developed and became very evident, which led to an eventual breakup. The key flaws that emerged were unfaithfulness, emotional instability, lack of career motivation and alcohol dependency. These problems probably were not obvious when the respondents were in their twenties or thirties. Such traits evolved over time. This points out the necessity for midlife men and women to spend time ferreting out any of these flaws that may exist in their potential partners. Ascertaining these deficiencies may not have been possible in youth, but it is now, so don't ignore the signs!

Breakups Are Still Mysterious

While it is true that most of us know ourselves better now than we did at age twenty, many of our respondents were still unclear about what they would have done differently to save their marriages or failed relationships. The fact that 31 percent of men and 35 percent of women still didn't understand how they could have saved their marriages or past relationships reinforces the concept that we need to be more introspective and spend time analyzing our needs and desires as well as those of our partners.

We wanted to know what people have learned, so we included this question in our survey: "What would you do differently in your next relationship?"

Men responded:	
I don't know	(31%)
take more time before making a commitment	(26%)
make a better choice	(18%)
communicate my feelings more clearly	(12%)
not dwell on negative aspects of the relationship	(8%)
give her more support	(5%)

One man told us, "I would make sure we played more. I always seemed to be working to get ahead and she was always busy with the children. We didn't take time to have much fun together and then it was too late."

The fact that almost 50 percent of men said they should have "taken more time" or should have "made a better choice" clearly reinforces the theme of this book, which is to use your newfound knowledge to learn all you can about a potential romantic partner.

The women's most frequently given answers corresponded to the men's in that they were unclear how they could have saved their relationship. Some 35 percent stated, "I don't know," which, quite surprisingly, seems to indicate women are even worse than men when it comes to evaluating past relationships.

Women responded:

I don't know	(35%)
be clearer on what I wanted	(24%)
not fall in love so quickly	(17%)
leave quickly when it's over	(12%)
maintain more independence	(9%)
not expect so much	(3%)

Although not in the category of what they would have done differently to save the marriage, many women (12 percent) simply said they wish they had left sooner when they realized the relationship was over. The fact that a total of 41 percent felt they could "be clearer about what they wanted" and felt they "fell in love too fast" would seem to indicate a good percentage of women will use their newfound knowledge about relationships to learn about potential mates before committing in the future.

The Changing Attitudes of Women Confuse Many Men

Many men and a fair percentage of women in our study agreed with the notion that, traditionally, women have been "support people" with little equality in decision making in relationships. This was primarily true of the generations that grew up in the 1940s, 1950s and even the early 1960s, when this attitude was prevalent. Then, most women and men essentially had pre-determined roles and the relationship was a scenario in which these roles were played out.

Attitudes have changed significantly over the past thirty-odd years. As these new attitudes became more prevalent, more and more women came to the conclusion that they wanted independence, regardless of what their husbands thought. In some cases, divorce was the result of women deciding the predetermined "support role" was no longer one they wanted to play.

In college, Marilee told Marshall all she wanted was to get married, have several kids, a nice house and garden. Marshall, in turn, thought this was exactly what he wanted and he soon proposed. They married the month after graduation, each at the ripe age of twenty-two. Thirty years later, when her next-door neighbor's administrative assistant got sick, Marilee agreed to help out for two weeks. Six years later, she is still there, in a rewarding and stimulating career. When Marshall occasionally asks, "Where are my clean shirts?" she cheerfully replies, "I have no idea."

Unlike Marshall, some men have been slow or often unwilling, to accept this change in women's attitudes. As a result, such men do not do well in starting new relationships when they encounter women with independent views. Many men, in trying to adjust to being single in the twenty-first century, will say, "Yes, I really want an independent woman," when in their hearts they know they cannot handle a woman with a strong mind of her own. Men may sincerely try to accept an independent woman, but in reality they cannot. This can be hard for a woman, dating a man who says he truly likes you as an independent person, but later finding he really cannot deal with this aspect of you. Both of you are in danger of falling deeply into the trap you may have just escaped.

Make Sure He "Gets It"

Observe what a man does when you have an alternative plan for an evening or a weekend. Does he discuss the alternative and agree or does he seem reluctant to listen or even seem aggravated about your idea? What happens during a discussion in which you disagree? Does he essentially disregard your ideas and thoughts or does he give you his attention and listen with a truly open mind to what you have to say? If you observe signs indicating the man is truly unable to cope with your independence of thought and action, do not ignore the signals. Be sure you do not rationalize and fall back into the same sort of relationship that was oppressive in the past.

Men, too, need to understand what their real attitude is about independent women and deal with it accordingly. A man should not try to adjust to an independent woman, just because she is new and exciting; the relationship won't last if the man still insists on being the dominant partner.

Two strong people with the right attitude toward one another can be mutually supportive and put each other first in the relationship. This works if the two people have a mature and unselfish love without a need for dominance.

Think It Through

First, decide what kind of relationship you want at this point in your life. Second, be clear about your own situation and the qualities that would make someone want you.

Let's say you have become a successful career person while maintaining a household as a single mother. If you aren't taking care of your kids, you are dealing with job situations and fellow employees. Out of necessity, you do everything for everybody else. You start to think it is high time you find someone to take care of you. But down deep, you know you really want an equal partner who respects your independence. This is truly a conundrum.

Such an attitude is a major trap that lures many women into the wrong type of relationship. If it didn't work before, it won't work now, so be sure the man with whom you decide to become involved can truly deal with you and respect your independence. Conversely, the man in this relationship needs to decide if he really wants a woman who has her own mind and a strong will that does not bend to his every desire and need.

Don't let the fear of loneliness or, alternatively, the newness or the excitement of dating again, blind you to the realities of a new relationship. To do so may put you right back in the cycle of negative past behavior that was not beneficial then and won't be now. You can now analyze the type of person you have become and decide whether you want to change your attitude and partner requirements. You had great excuses when you were in your twenties and didn't really understand what real equality in a relationship meant. Who did? Understand what you now want in a partner. Don't be mesmerized by the same attributes you ultimately found undesirable in your past relationship.

Don't Assume

Three stories of people in our study illustrate conflicting views of people who got what they thought they wanted and then learned it did not work for them.

Anne had always wanted a successful man and was thrilled when she began a relationship with a CEO of a startup company. However, she hated the fact that he worked twelve hours a day and most weekends. Anne slowly realized she needed a partner—even if he was less successful—who could spend more time with her. The relationship ended after two years. Luckily, they had not married.

Likewise, Donald, a building contractor, was very proud of Carla, a top negotiator for a company engaged in large scale corporate business leasing. He thought she was the most alive and exciting person he had ever known and was very happy when, after a long courtship, they moved in together. But soon, Donald found her international travel to be disconcerting. He had expected that Carla would make changes in her work life and be home more often once they lived together. Wrong! Donald had a very difficult and painful process untangling himself from her, but felt he had to do it. He told us, "Fifty-two percent of the time I know I made the right decision, but the other forty-eight percent of the time, I just do not know. It still hurts and I sometimes wonder if I could have made it work. But in my heart, I know Carla could not give me what I wanted."

Betty was dating Arnold and considering marriage. She had always been religious, but had not communicated to Arnold how important her faith was to her. When Betty finally told Arnold she wanted to stop working when they married and become more involved in church activities, she learned for the first time that Arnold actually had his heart set on buying a house in a small community over one hundred miles away. This revelation made Betty realize just how important her church had become to her. Amazingly, Betty had not thought to tell Arnold about her strong religious preference and her attachment to her church community, assuming this would not be a problem.

She now realizes she will not settle for anyone who is not as committed as she to the church and she will not make the mistake of failing to communicate this fact to any potential partner. She has come to believe that everything else is secondary to her faith. Betty and Arnold ended their relationship. Luckily, they found out in time that their needs were incompatible and prevented what would have been a disastrous situation.

Decide What Is Important

There are other characteristics and attitudes that may be subtle, but which will impact you one way or another. They may or may not be the deal killers just described, but whether you are new to dating or you are a true veteran of the Middle Game, it is very important to learn what you don't know about yourself and make the most of the strengths and weaknesses you possess. What do you like in a man or a woman? What qualities do you have that would make them want you? What are your "must have" qualities and what are your "can't deal with" qualities in the opposite sex? Few of us have ever really made this analysis, but it is essential to know what makes you interested (or not) and what things you like and dislike in a partner. A few areas that could cause concern are outlined in the following paragraphs. Are they important to you?

Sloppiness Can Kill a Relationship

Many women in our study expressed consistent dismay at a behavioral trait of many men they had dated, namely, the men's seeming inability to pick up their clothes or keep their living quarters in at least some rudimentary state of neatness. Hence, a big tip for men: When you find a woman who is interested in you and you decide to take her to your home, be sure it is presentable. Few women are inclined toward romance when they see you cannot take care of your own basic needs. This also applies in reverse. A man who, on a first visit to a woman's home, finds boxes and "collectibles" in every corner may be inclined to wonder about the disorganization he encounters.

Keep Your Ailments to Yourself

A habit that seems to come with maturity for some men is discussing, at length, their ailments. Since men often don't have many physical problems when they are younger, there can be a tendency to discuss these newfound ailments with their dates. It's a novelty for some men, almost like a kid with a new toy: "I have a prostate problem; I have a bad back; my knees are giving me trouble." Men also have these same discussions with one another, which is one reason why it seems natural to them to have these same discussions with women. For some reason, men feel women will be sympathetic, interested and comforting.

Wrong! For your information, gentlemen, most women do not consider any of these things the least bit interesting. They will undoubtedly be thinking, "The sooner my date with this broken down man is over, the better."

Of course, women can fall into the same trap. Nancy goes to lunch each month with five of her best women friends. Halfway through a recent luncheon, she burst out laughing as she realized that for nearly an hour all they had talked about were their various new health problems. Now they have a firm rule: At the beginning of their lunches, each woman gets one minute to summarize her health issues (yes, it is timed) and from then on, they have agreed not to mention the boring subject of health again!

Ask Your Friends

How do you plan ahead to avoid these and many other rookie dating game errors? Many men and women have found, for example, that their good friends or even former partners with whom they have had close relationships can be some of the best sources for constructive criticism about improvement and self-awareness. Who knows you better than someone you may have dated or lived with for many years?

Indeed, you are likely to get your best advice from a friend of the opposite sex. There is much less inhibition in being open when men talk to women and women talk to men. There are clearly exceptions to this, Nancy, for example, thinks a close woman friend, a "sister at heart," will open up in a unique way and be very forthright. She has always relied on women friends for candid and frank feedback as well as constructive advice.

Hopefully, you are lucky enough to have someone in your life, male or female, who will tell you at least some of your bad traits. Mason recently asked the help of a woman he had lived with for seven years and came up with a basic list of qualities he possessed that a woman would probably find attractive. With the help of the same woman, Mason created a list of his bad qualities. Based on these evaluations, it became clear that he needs to change some areas of his life in order to have any chance at long-term success in a relationship. He also learned what qualities he has that he should accentuate. Nancy too recently made a list of her positives and negatives with the help of her friends and, in doing so, reached valuable conclusions about herself and what she needs in a potential partner.

The bonus in doing this exercise is that it can facilitate communication in your next relationship. People tend to understand and be supportive when they know you are being truthful with them about your faults (as long as they are not so outrageous and undesirable that you seem unredeemable). They are also glad to know you are aware of them and working to improve yourself. You should have a close friend help you create your own list and see if there are any egregious flaws you may need to work on to improve your sociability quotient.

Make a List

It is important for both men and women to spend some time self-evaluating and determining which things need to be changed in their basic approach to the opposite sex. Everyone needs at least some minor "fine tuning." If you think you are totally acceptable as you are you, it is probably a mistaken assumption. You need to ask yourself from time to time, "Why would someone want me?" And you need to be clear and realistic with yourself about the answers. The bad traits you have developed over the past twenty or thirty years may not have been articulated to you, but merely tolerated by your former spouse or partner.

Making a list of three of your best features and three of your correctable faults is a good start. Discuss with your friend why you come across this way and share recommendations for future corrections. Then mark your calendar for a six-month follow up session when you can candidly discuss your progress.

This leads to one other related issue that was touched on earlier: When in new encounters, ask key questions about lifestyles, attitudes, and beliefs sooner rather than later. It's okay to be straightforward and use your knowledge and experience to evaluate your date. Be judgmental, it's your life and it is not advantageous at this point to be wasteful of your time.

Although not dating related, one woman in our study, Paula, told us about a situation at work that was similar to this effort to highlight positive and negative traits. Paula had been generous in handing out advice and giving honest feedback to a new woman hired by her company and who reported to her. She was a good worker, but had no social graces. She interrupted meetings, talked too loudly, dressed inappropriately and had a raucous, grating laugh. Paula took her aside and worked closely with her to correct (or at least tone down) these problems.

The new employee took the suggestions to heart and worked hard to catch on quickly. Imagine Paula's feelings when a year later the new employee leap-frogged over Paula and was selected for promotion. Paula initially wondered if her desire to help her fellow worker backfired and actually weakened her position in the company. She later realized, as do all self-assured and confident people, that her time would come and she had done the right thing.

The Results Will Be Amazing

When we have lived into our middle years or later, we have, hopefully, developed a far greater understanding of our own strengths and weaknesses and, if we have been observant, those of the opposite sex as well. We should know what we want as well as what we cannot accept. We need to be clear about what we have to offer in a relationship and why someone would want us. It takes a mature person to be able to accept constructive criticism regarding his or her own weaknesses, yet this is necessary if we want to continue growing. A self-evaluation will go a long way in making sure others will be attracted to us.

As Shakespeare so aptly said, "To thine own self be true." With this in mind, search for someone with similar traits, beliefs, attitudes and social values to help you move forward in your new life. You now have the power to create a world you enjoy.

Quiz – Chapter 15

We change as we reach midlife and we have a much clearer understanding of ourselves. This quick quiz will help you evaluate why someone would want you. Please rate yourself:

10 points for a "yes"; 5 points for an "undecided"; 0 points for a "no."

Ranking   Question

_____   1. I can list three of my best traits.
_____   2. I can list three of my worst traits.
_____   3. I know the "must have" and "can't deal with" qualities I am looking for in my partner.
_____   4. I am willing to try to change the qualities my partner believes are deal killers.
_____   5. I understand why my last marriage/relationship failed.
_____   6. My friends and I spend time discussing our health and how it has changed, but we don't do it around our dates.
_____   7. I know I have worthwhile qualities and I am clear why someone would want me.

Scoring
70 – 60 - Sounds like you have it pretty well figured out!
50 – 30 - You have a good understanding of why the past did not work for you.
20 – 0   - Focus on the good qualities you have, as well as fixing some of the others.

PART 3

The End Game: Making Final Choices

Introduction

In backgammon, the end game (bearing your men off the board) requires less decision making than the Middle Game. In fact, the professional player has studied the computer analysis of all of the potential moves and has them memorized, thereby minimizing the need for further strategy or decisions. While the End Game of dating is not quite so precise, it is very similar—the decisions are reasonably clear-cut. First, you may be convinced that this is "the one." You now think you are serious about the man or woman you have been dating and you are in the final stages of deciding what to do about it. So what is your plan? Just as in any other life endeavor, there needs to be a focused strategy to get where you want to go and an end game plan that must be understood and executed.

During the End Game, there probably will be a point in time when the man or the woman you have been seeing wants to make the relationship an exclusive one. As we described earlier in our backgammon discussion, you must make a decision to stay and agree to exclusivity or decline the offer and drop out of the relationship. This section will describe how many of our survey participants responded to this challenge, as well as give examples of the outcome of their stay or drop decisions.

The issues are much more straightforward when you arrive at the End Game. All the relationship decisions of early adulthood have been made and you no longer have to reconcile such overwhelming earlier issues as: Do we want children and, if so, how many? Will they inherit any negative health problems? Will my partner be a good father/mother? Should we both work? How do we deal with in-laws one of us doesn't like? Will my partner be successful and make the necessary income to allow us to have a lifestyle we will enjoy? These problems, which have caused many marriages to crumble, are now, literally, history.

The End Game issues affecting those in midlife are very different. They center on health, retirement income, beliefs and deal-killer personality traits. Where do we want to live? Do we agree upon a pre-nuptial agreement? Is there a fatal flaw in my partner that I just can't reconcile? At this point, with the proper groundwork done, you should be able to make a relatively simple prediction about what the future holds for you and the person you have been dating.

In the final analysis, you must make that all-important decision about how you want the relationship to continue and how you both can stay happy and grow together. We may not seem that much different now than we were twenty or thirty years ago, but we are different, so it is more crucial than ever to make a decision about the relationship. The clock is running and the future is a shorter time period than before. It's decision time; you can't wait around for tomorrow—it is tomorrow! The End Game signifies "make a decision." Trust your instincts (which at this age should be relatively good); if you believe you are in love and there are no significant negatives to the relationship, it is probably better to stay than to drop.

So now that you have met this special person, you need to consider all of the options and make the right decision for both of you. But do not let the relationship end because of an outsized ego or an unwillingness to compromise—you could spend the rest of your life regretting it.

This section will assist you in making the stay or drop decision. It will clarify changing attitudes and will discuss the many new and exciting options we now have that may be in direct contrast with the idealistic and now outdated views of our youth. It will help you deal with past rejections and illustrate how others have turned a negative experience into a positive force. Once you have selected your partner and you decide to join together on a more permanent basis, you need to decide what that means. The practical decisions abound: Do you get married, live together or live apart and continue the relationship as it is? If marriage is not the end result, we will show examples of other options that can still make the relationship work. Finally, is this person your soulmate or does the concept even exist for people in midlife or older? Once you have made these final decisions—the dating game is over!

CHAPTER 16

The Stay or Drop Decision

"I finally learned what was important and I reluctantly realized I did not want my relationship to end because of an unwillingness to compromise."

Sarah

In backgammon, the doubling cube is used to force an opponent to make a decision to stay in the game and double the bet or concede. If you concede, you lose the bet for that game and you must start another game. In fact, as we noted in this section's introduction, a basic premise of winning at backgammon is knowing when to stay and when to drop. This is also true when you are in the End Game of dating.

Determine Where You Stand

Arriving at a clear understanding of where you stand in a relationship and then making the decision to stay or drop is an apt strategy for dating. It is important to analyze your position and cut your losses, if you determine the relationship is not going anywhere, even if you have successfully completed the Middle Game. Of course, this often is easier said than done. It is always hard to break off a relationship, particularly one that has gone on for a significant period of time and has been highly satisfying in many ways. It is hard to reconcile the fact that you have wasted all that energy and emotion. So the key question becomes: Is it necessary? Well, maybe yes and maybe no. There are some situations in which no amount of rationalization is going to change what you intuitively know—it's over. Other situations are not so clear-cut.

"Commitment" Is a Word That Needs Defining

It is important for you to decide just what commitment means to you. Does commitment mean marriage, living together or being totally monogamous and dedicated to one another while living apart?

You may be in a situation in which your partner is having two or more simultaneous dating relationships. You may well be the one truly loved, but he or she either is unsure of your affection or not sure it's time to make a total commitment. Maybe your partner is just having a good time and not feeling pressed to make a decision about anything permanent. Just because he or she is dating others does not mean your partner does not believe you are, or at least could be, the one. But if you have doubts about the future of your relationship with this individual, it is up to *you* to make the decision to stay or drop.

Consider All Your Options before Deciding

Before you make a hasty, emotional decision to drop, consider Jackie's experience. Jackie was dating Jason, who was also dating another woman. When Jackie made this discovery, she was hurt that he could do such a thing and her first inclination was to break off the relationship. She promptly did this without so much as a discussion with him. Within two months, Jason married the other woman he was dating.

Jackie happened to meet this woman at a party a few months later and asked her how she managed to get Jason to settle down and marry her. She responded, "I told him he had to make a decision—no other women or I was gone. He said, 'Okay,' and within about two weeks he asked me to marry him." Jackie told us, "I didn't think about handling it in that manner. I just made the immediate decision to cut the relationship off. I guess I should have given him an ultimatum and seen how he responded." Indeed, she should have, so before you make precipitous decisions (assuming this is an individual you want) don't be a Jackie, just ask for what you want! Anyone in sales will recognize this as the simple, but all-important lesson that many salespeople must learn: Ask for the order.

Don't Overreact with Jealousy to a Past Incident

There will be some point at which your partner tells you about his or her past experiences with other women or men. Sometimes this even happens on the first date! This can be good because it creates a trusting environment. Some of you will be much more forthcoming than others and the stories may be very explicit. There is nothing wrong with elaborating on your past and it is a good sign of honesty and openness to your partner, but you need to judge the best time to share the details and where to stop.

For example, even if you have had a busy and fruitful dating career, you do not want to tell your new partner how many people you have slept with. People often have a tendency to forget that the past is the past. In fact, when some people hear a story about a past love, they think of it as just happening yesterday, even though it may have been years earlier.

If your partner shares his or her past romantic experiences with you, accept such stories for what they are—history. Retroactive jealousy is a very bad trait that can easily destroy a relationship. Do not let past experiences your partner had with another man or woman cause you to drop. This is worth repeating: Do not let stories about past relationships affect your present relationship. This should not even cause you to get to the level of making a stay or drop decision.

There is, however, one form of retroactive jealousy that should cause you to consider dropping. On-going jealousy by your new partner, based on the fact you are still friendly with a former wife, husband or lover, is a problem. This kind of jealousy is probably indicative of low self-esteem, which makes any former partner of yours seemingly a threat. By now you should know this kind of attitude or response is not healthy for a long-term relationship where trust is essential. A drop would certainly seem to be in order as this attitude seldom improves.

A Healthy Dialogue between Secure People

Hugh and Elaine are an example of two people in a healthy relationship. Elaine enjoyed hearing about his past experiences with other women, saying she found his stories interesting and often humorous. When they went out and Hugh said "hello" to another woman, Elaine wanted to know if she was someone he had been out with and when. Clearly Elaine did not suffer from low self-esteem. She knew the past was the past and she did not have any objection to his remaining friends with his past lovers. She actually found the women very companionable and, in fact, became friends with two of them.

Remember, You're an Adult Now

This philosophy directly contrasts with the advice frequently given by some psychologists, which states all communication must be severed with a past love and any on-going relationship with him or her will lead to future disaster with your next partner. We think this concept flies in the face of adult logic and is either directed solely toward very immature people or is an indication they have not had healthy past relationships. Anyone with practical, healthy, life experiences with the opposite sex will tell you that maintaining communication with your former spouses or lovers can be very fulfilling and is the sign of maturity. This is especially true if you share children with a past partner.

What Matters to You?

Duane is an example of someone in an unhealthy situation. His relationship with his partner, Georgia, was the opposite of Hugh's. If he dared mention any former woman friend, or even stopped to have a conversation with a woman he knew, Georgia would immediately want to know what was going on and, in a confrontational manner, want to know the exact nature of the past relationship. She was clearly insecure about their relationship and felt threatened by any past romantic experiences on the part of Duane. Even though Duane had been in a relationship with Georgia for more than two years and been faithful during this time, she still did not trust him. He learned never to bring up the subject of other women who had been in his life. He stayed in the relationship, feeling that her attitude, while very insecure, was something he could live with since they were compatible in so many other ways.

Over time, however, Duane grew weary of having to work so hard at handling Georgia's jealousy of his past relationships. At last report, Duane was busy complaining to his best friend about his inability to continually have to deal with Georgia's insecurities. He was strongly considering a drop.

Can You Wait It Out? Do You Want To?

Melody had been dating Bryan for seven years. Although they saw each other two or three times a week and constantly traveled together, Bryan, who had been married for almost thirty years prior to dating Melody, still couldn't resist the allure of other women. Melody was aware of Bryan's dalliances, but made the decision that she was having a wonderful time and she was in love with him. She decided to wait out Bryan's other ventures, rather than create a confrontation. Last year they were married and Bryan has become a loyal partner. Melody's decision to overlook behavior she didn't like and wait for Bryan to move beyond his womanizing is not something everyone can live with, but it worked for her.

Bryan later explained that one of the key reasons he eventually opted for a monogamous life with Melody was the fact that she did not interrogate him constantly about where he had been each day he didn't see her and didn't pressure him to change. This works both ways. When the situation is reversed, men should not constantly query a woman about her activities when she is not with him. It is a quality that highlights your personal insecurity and can only be seen as negative by the other person.

The contrasting situations of Duane and Georgia and Melody and Bryan say one thing: While you need to do what your own belief system tells you, don't make decisions that may cut off what could turn out to be a happy ending. All these situations represent, to use our backgammon analogy, a doubling cube situation, in which a decision had to be made to take the cube and stay in the game (with its obviously higher emotional stakes) or drop and start a new one. It is never a simple black and white decision. In your twenties or thirties there were lots of options and there frequently was a new person waiting right around the corner. But now you aren't thirty...

Making the Right Decision for You

Connie, who is fifty-eight, had dated Dwight for eight years. While they had separate houses, they were together about five nights a week. Both had a passion for golf and they frequently traveled together to golfing resorts. The problem? Dwight lived with his mother who was ninety-one and in poor health.

Dwight did not feel he could leave the elderly woman and kept reminding Connie of the promise he had made to his father (just before his father died) that he would always take care of his mother. Eventually, Dwight's mother passed away. What happened? Dwight still did not want to get married. Connie felt hurt, betrayed and angry, because she had not seen the signs that he simply did not want to be married. In her case, she felt she lost eight years in which she could have been looking for a marriage partner, which was her goal. What do you think? Should she have dropped Dwight sooner? Is it that important to be married if the relationship is otherwise good?

On the other hand, Kitty is a forty-seven-year-old woman who has decided to stay in a relationship with Milt. Milt is a handsome and charming man who is completely devoted to Kitty. The problem? Milt has very little money and no ambition to further himself. In addition, he told Kitty he really didn't feel he could ever marry again, because he so cherished his independence. He works for a bank and is a few years away from retirement, but has been unable to accumulate any significant savings.

After several months of courtship, Kitty invited Milt to move into her beautiful six-bedroom home in a prestigious area. He immediately settled into her comfortable lifestyle and began enjoying the activities at her exclusive club. As he had before, he continued to cater to Kitty's every whim. He brought her coffee in bed every morning along with the papers. When Kitty compared Milt to many of her friends' husbands, she saw him as being relatively unsuccessful in his career and not as socially polished as she would prefer, but he adored her and to Kitty that meant a lot. She made a conscious decision to never drop this wonderful man who made such a great effort to make her happy. Milt seems like a lucky guy to have Kitty and her resources taking care of him, but Kitty is very fortunate, also, to be loved and treated so well. What do you think? Would a relationship like this work for you?

No One Said It's Easy, But You Need to Be Decisive

In your forties, fifties and beyond, there is not necessarily a new person waiting for you right around the corner. As we get older, we are all much less open to people who don't fit into our belief systems and we have a much smaller window of opportunity for finding truly compatible partners. It's just another statistical reality of which we must be cognizant in midlife.

The question that needs to be answered at some point becomes: Is this man or woman ever going to commit to anyone ? And, if so, is there any chance you are going to be the one? Again, the analogy to backgammon is appropriate. When you are challenged to accept the double cube or drop the game, all of your emotions are to stay and accept the cube. To drop is incredibly emotionally difficult.

You would be amazed at how long it sometimes takes and how agonizing it is for backgammon players to make this decision in an actual game. It is also amazing how many decide not to drop even when the odds are overwhelmingly against them and it's obvious they should start another game. Backgammon and relationships have this in common: Emotions rule.

Understand a Previous Drop

It is useful to have a perspective on why each of your prior relationships ended. While not necessarily a major determinant in making a decision, it may be a useful guide to understanding your current partner. Our curiosity about this issue led us to include this question in our survey: "Why did your most recent relationship or marriage end?" We decided not to include death in our analysis, but noted with regret that 18 percent of the women and 12 percent of the men lost relationships due to the end of their partners' lives.

```
Men responded:
    Drifted apart                    (32%)
    Poor communication               (24%)
    Problems within family           (17%)
    Goals became divergent           (14%)
    She had to be right              (10%)
    She wanted to raise
        grandchildren, I did not      (3%)
```

```
Women responded:
    Drifted Apart                    (26%)
    He had an affair, flame
        went out                     (24%)
    He was too controlling           (21%)
    Put his interests ahead of mine  (15%)
    Financial priorities differed    (12%)
    He was immature; did not
        want to grow up               (2%)
```

Do any of these responses correspond with reasons you might have given for the end of a relationship?

Drop with Class

If you have decided that now is the time to drop rather than go forward with the relationship, there are a couple of things you need to do. First, don't make the drop acrimonious, because that doesn't do anything for anyone. Why waste the energy? Granted this may be difficult as you presumably are emotionally involved, but steel your mind, keep your cool and just do it. Second, don't spend time worrying about what might have been. Accept that it's just over. You need to do the best you can to put all of the negative thoughts out of your mind. And third, don't speak negatively to others about your former partner. That is not only unproductive, but reflects very badly on you since it makes you look petty and insecure.

Be Firm and Have the Courage of Your Convictions

Because some women do not like the emotional trauma that comes with a breakup, they may tend toward recycling the same man. Time and time again, a man will try to weasel his way back into the life of a woman with statements like, "I won't do it again" or "I'll change" or other such standard slogans. Women, often because this represents the path of least resistance and is the known versus the unknown, will frequently submit to these pleas for forgiveness.

That Commitment Thing Again

There is yet one more scenario. If you feel your partner is really dedicated to you and you are having a wonderful time, do you really care if there has not been an official "commitment?" And just what is a commitment and without one do you really need to make the drop decision? The following is a story about just such a situation. You be the judge as to what Sarah should have done.

After eighteen months of dating Josh, Sarah, who was fifty-two, decided it was time to take action. She wanted to move the absolutely great relationship she was experiencing with Josh, who was the same age, to the next level. But after all of this time, Sarah was not having success in getting Josh to commit to marriage, which she desperately wanted. Yet they were constant companions— traveling, skiing, playing tennis—and they saw each other at least four days (and nights) a week. They did not live together on a full time basis, but were about as close as you get without taking that step. However, Sarah was grounded in the traditional thinking of marriage as the only true commitment.

In frustration, she resorted to the classic absence-makes-the-heart grow-fonder strategy, often used successfully by people in their twenties when everyone is somewhat inexperienced and insecure. Although this is a ploy that has gained credibility from some quarters, in fact, it rarely works with the mature and experienced segment of the population. Sarah's strategy was to make him really want her by absenting herself from his life. Usually, such a plan entails not seeing or talking to the other person for a period of time. More drastically, Sarah decided to move away.

Sarah called her good friend and confidant, Wayne, and told him she had decided to break up with Josh. She said although he was probably going to ask her to live with him, he was not going to marry her. Sarah had decided this was unacceptable.

Wayne asked, "Are you happy?"

Sarah answered, "Yes."

"Is there something Josh does that you do not like?"

"No."

"So what is the problem?"

"He won't marry me and I need to be married. I have decided to break it off and move to Los Angeles."

Wayne counseled that this strategy would not work. Josh, who Wayne also knew, was not going to run to Los Angeles and try to persuade Sarah to come back. She would be living a miserable life in a new city in which she would essentially restart her life at the age of fifty-two.

The result was that Sarah moved and Josh didn't come running after her. In fact, he had a new woman friend within two months. Sarah stayed in Los Angeles six months, realized her plan had backfired and moved back to Denver, where she has been unable to find a man with all of Josh's qualities. Nice plan, but it didn't work and Sarah went from a near-perfect relationship to an imperfect life in the blink of an eye.

Sarah now spends a great deal of time trying to get back to where she started and resume her relationship with Josh where they left off, minus her demand for marriage. In fact, she has totally changed her view on marriage and now says, while it still would be desirable in the long run, she no longer considers it mandatory to a relationship. In her words, she has "finally learned what is important."

So if your relationship is perfect, or almost perfect, consider the alternative before you act hastily and end up in never-never land. And, if you absolutely must try the "absence makes the heart grow fonder" ploy, don't move, just stop seeing the other person for a while. Don't wait too long, though. If it appears not to be working, get back in the game as soon as possible.

Stay or Drop is a Complex Decision

Karen and Roy had been living together for several months and planned to get married eventually. Roy enjoyed competing in bowling tournaments, which occurred almost every weekend, with many being held in other states. For practice, he bowled in two different leagues each week.

Roy was handsome, smart and charming, but he always seemed to put himself and his strenuous bowling schedule first. This made him miss countless birthdays, family celebrations and other activities that Karen thought important. Karen soon realized she and her needs would never come first with Roy and she regretfully decided to drop him.

Weston dated Maureen for nine years, escorting her to functions and acting as a jack-of-all-trades repairman in her lovely home. He also was instrumental in helping her twenty-one-year-old son kick his drug habit. Weston knew Maureen occasionally had dates with other men, but try as he might, Weston could not get her to make a total commitment to him. While this tore him up emotionally, he didn't think he could ever again find anyone he wanted or loved as much. He decided not to drop the relationship, no matter what the costs. His life, in order to work, simply needed Maureen in it.

Glen, a sixty-three-year-old man, was in an unhappy marriage of twenty-five years and considering a divorce. He knew the divorce would cause a major financial disruption and force him to dramatically change his lifestyle. For this reason, he had been procrastinating. However, he changed his mind and, despite the turmoil it will create, is moving ahead with the divorce.

When asked why he had the change of heart, his comment was, "It dawned on me that I am now in my sixties, and even though I don't feel it and don't look it, I'm no youngster. If I don't make a move now and I wait a few more years before starting a new life and trying to find a new relationship, it's going to be too late. I know I want to be in a loving relationship and trying to meet a woman and start all over when I am seventy would be just that much more difficult. I need to do it now." This is the kind of drop decision that is excruciatingly hard to make and many would not be able to make the decision Glen made.

There comes a time in all relationships when you need to make the stay or drop decision. Most relationships are not perfect and this choice can be an emotionally tough one, fraught with tension and strong feelings. Once you are in the End Game, you realize how much time and emotion have been invested. Therefore, the benefits and drawbacks of the relationship need to be weighed very, very carefully. But with your many years of experience, you are now far better equipped to evaluate the options and make a decision that you will be happy with for the rest of your life.

Quiz – Chapter Sixteen

The End Game has fewer decisions than the Beginning or Middle Games, but they are among the most important that you will ever make. As in backgammon, the time comes to "stay" or "drop." This quick quiz will help you evaluate this emotionally tough choice. Please rate yourself as follows:

10 points for a "yes"; 5 points for an "undecided"; 0 points for a "no"

Ranking Question

_____ 1. I have made these difficult emotional decisions before.

_____ 2. I understand the consequence of a decision at this point in my life.

_____ 3. I am clear about what I want in a final relationship.

_____ 4. If a relationship is unhealthy and not in my best interest, I have the courage to end it, no matter what.

_____ 5. I am not jealous of my partner's past relationships.

_____ 6. If the most important goal in my life is to get married, I know I may have to force the issue and not wait for years to see if my partner commits.

_____ 7. If I was dropped, I would accept it. I have the capacity to move on with my life and get back in the game within a reasonable amount of time.

Scoring

70 – 60 - You are able to make healthy and mature decisions in the End Game.

50 – 30 - You seem aware of the consequences of any decision.

20 – 0   - Think and be sure of your decision, then learn to continue with no regrets.

CHAPTER 17

Changing Attitudes, New Options

"My number one goal? To find a partner and be in a lasting relationship."
Gilda

"**I** DON'T WANT TO GET MARRIED!" This is a statement heard and said time and time again by both men and women. Many of our study participants told us, "I have been there, done that and I don't want to get back into that kind of a relationship. I am certainly interested in having a partner and I would live with someone, but I will not get married again."

Do They Really Mean What They Say?

There are some people who really mean this when they say it, but our research indicates they are in the minority by far. Almost everyone who says they do not want to get married will do an absolute one hundred and eighty degree turn and walk down the aisle if the right person shows up at his or her doorstep. But if you are in a situation in which your partner is absolutely adamant about not marrying or there are legal or financial complications that prevent it, must you end the relationship? Assuming all else is wonderful, definitely not. Be creative and come up with a relationship structure that works for you both.

There are, of course, exceptions. Bart, one of the men in our study, usually tells his partners early in the relationships that he doesn't plan to marry. Bart is a high achiever and dates women who have similar traits.

According to him, many women who are also high achievers and who have strong self-images often enjoy a challenge and Bart had the feeling several women vigorously pursued him just to see if they could get him to change his mind. So far, that hasn't happened, but he did say if the right one appears, he would marry her. Of course, only Bart knows if that is true.

Mary Lou told us with humorous cynicism, "I never married, because there was no need. I have three pets at home that serve the same purpose as a husband. I have a dog that growls at me every morning, a parrot that swears at me at the end of the day and a cat that either comes home late at night or not at all!" While Mary Lou is clearly suspicious of men, she stated she would, in fact, welcome a man into her life if he possessed her ideal traits.

Never Say Never

Netta swore, "I am never going to marry again!" She was one of the many women in our study who were (or once were) emphatic about remaining unattached. She went on to become a perfect example of finding her own Returning Veteran, by marrying her high school boyfriend, Keith, who lived in Santa Fe. She married him despite having told him for two years she was absolutely not interested in getting married again. Not only did she marry him, but as you will recall from her story, she moved from New York City to Santa Fe to be with him.

Mason was invited to her wedding in Santa Fe (remember one of the basic rules: Remain friends with former partners) and witnessed one of the most romantic weddings he had ever attended. Keith actually wrote and read a poem describing his long wait for Netta, thereby causing every woman in the audience to break into tears and proving that romantic men do exist.

Bear in mind that it is a relatively good bet that anyone who states unequivocally that he or she will never get married again probably will. If you are the one who is interested in being married to the person espousing this kind of rhetoric, just have patience. And don't make an ill-advised and drastic maneuver as Sarah did when she moved to Los Angeles to force the issue. Even if you don't marry, the relationship is what is important. Find a way to make it work and don't let a tradition-bound mindset get in the way.

Should Age Differences Matter?

An interesting example of how attitudes change as we mature emerged from our study. Men and women both stated that in their twenties they wanted to marry someone within three years of their age. Now, however, they indicate they would consider a much wider age range. Women reported they would prefer to date men no more than seven years younger and eight years older, while men said they would prefer to date women up to fifteen years younger, but no more than three years older. The good news is that being in your middle years or older opens up a much wider range of new options for a partner. The men's professed unwillingness to date women significantly older, however, clearly reflects their unfortunate preoccupation with youth.

When asked what the difference in age was in their best relationship, 86 percent of the men said their partners were younger, with the difference being an average of 8.6 years between them. Eighty-one percent of the women stated that their partners were older with the average age difference being 5.1 years. This means 19 percent of the women have had great relationships with younger men and 14 percent of the men had their best relationships with older women. These statistics throw cold water on the myth that older men are mainly interested in relationships with very young women. It would appear that while men say they wouldn't date women more than three years older than themselves, if the right woman shows up, a significant number of men will not allow the age difference to get in the way of a happy and fulfilling relationship.

Priorities Change

To gauge changing attitudes, we asked "What are your personal goals for the future?" We got answers that clearly reflect what people feel about themselves as they age.

Men said:	
find a partner	(34%)
stay healthy	(24%)
live an active life	(16%)
keep learning	(11%)
become more footloose	(7%)
help others	(4%)
be happy	(4%)

It may be news to the many women who think most men are commitment phobic, but 34 percent of our male respondents indicated, "finding a partner" is their number one goal. Interestingly, this is an even higher percentage than that stated by women. The goals of "staying healthy" and "active" reflect the reality that with age come certain necessary priorities and also reinforce the theme of the book, which is that time is no longer on your side when it comes to waiting around for something to happen. It's doubtful anyone would have listed these as primary goals in their twenties or even thirties—being healthy and active was assumed.

```
Women said:
    find a safe, secure relationship   (32%)
    be healthy                         (17%)
    financial security                 (15%)
    live a long life                   (12%)
    personal growth                    (10%)
    make a difference                   (8%)
    follow a spiritual path             (6%)
```

Note both men and women stated their number one goal is to find a partner and be in a relationship. Also significant is the fact that both genders said staying healthy was their number two goal. In fact, mature men's and women's goals tend to be very similar, with the exception that a significant percentage of women are looking for financial security. This probably reflects the fact that a number of women now in their mature years married young, became homemakers and didn't get the opportunity to pursue careers.

The choice of "following a spiritual path," was the surprising answer of 6 percent of the female respondents. This may reflect the need of many women to find peace within themselves after the end of a marriage or long-term relationship, or, perhaps, it may be the result of midlife and older women now having the time and opportunity to follow a more introspective and fulfilling path. In fact, the corresponding answer for men, with a 7 percent total, was to "become more footloose," an answer that could be interpreted as being almost diametrically opposed to women becoming spiritual. Clearly, these two groups are unlikely to be compatible.

Full Disclosure Solidifies the Relationship

One of the great benefits of being mature and experienced is that we have some basic knowledge about what we are good at and what are our faults. The ability to recognize these and be up front about them can only help a good relationship survive and flourish. For example, Netta and Keith will most probably stay together. Why? Because there will be no surprises—they each know the other's good and bad points.

Mason, who once dated Netta, said she had an occasional tendency to sort of "flip out" and assert one point or another in a verbally aggressive fashion. It was so intense that Mason usually just retreated into silence. Mason nicknamed this tendency the Netta "going bad" syndrome. They parted ways and remained close friends, so so when Mason saw she was nearing the stage where she and Keith were very serious, he asked her if Keith had experienced her "going bad" as yet. She said, "Yes, he has, and he still likes me. I even forewarned him it would happen so he wouldn't be totally shocked." This is not the kind of communication that would have occurred when Netta and Keith were in their twenties or thirties; it is a product of the maturity and knowledge about ourselves that comes with age.

You Can Modify Behavior, But There Are Limits

As you may have learned in your first marriage or long-term relationship, you can't change ingrained traits or drastically alter the bad habits of others. It is possible, however, to modify behavior. For example, you might get someone to go to a symphony with you even though he or she has never done that before or you might get someone to give up an old out-of-style tie or suit in favor of something more modern, but these are relatively minor adjustments. Usually, basic personalities or ingrained habits cannot be budged.

Cynthia loved everything about her partner, Jim, except for his sometimes-slovenly look. Jim is retired and spends a lot of time in outdoor activities, so most of the time his casual, outdated clothes didn't matter. But Cynthia was genuinely embarrassed when they went to social functions, to the point that she was about to call off their relationship. Finally, after a heart-to-heart talk, she got Jim to go shopping with her and together they picked out some new clothes for him. While he was not especially enthused over the new additions to his wardrobe, he agreed to wear them when he accompanied Cynthia on social occasions, because he knew how much it meant to her.

When a good relationship is at stake, sensible people opt to make changes. Steve had a tendency to view women only as sexual objects until he met Shirley, who won his heart. He immediately modified his behavior to that of a caring partner who teaches Shirley tennis, takes her for walks on the beach, cooks for her, takes her to family events and is highly attentive. To his friends, this was an unbelievable turnabout, but Steve's love for Shirley caused him to modify his behavior. He willingly and enthusiastically made the change.

Sometimes an ingrained, long-term habit can be changed, assuming the person really wants to change. Alcoholics can stop drinking and smokers can stop smoking, but the impetus to change must come from within. Overweight and out of shape people who have health problems may be convinced to exercise and eat properly (heart attacks and strokes are good "automatic" behavior modifiers), particularly if they perceive the alternative to be disability or even death. You can help a partner make changes, but the motivation must come from within the individual.

Sometimes You're Just Out of Luck

If your partner yells at people, is argumentative, has no sense of humor, has volatile personality traits and a quick temper, has a negative, complaining attitude or treats waiters and other service people with disdain, you may have to accept that this is probably the way he or she is now and will be in the future. You either have to accept those traits or drop the person. Hopefully, most of us have learned the futility of trying to change ingrained behavior. How many people married someone thinking, "Well, I can change that personality trait or habit once we are married." It probably didn't work then; don't be fooled into thinking it will work now. It won't.

Opting for a Lifestyle

Jillian confessed she was considering a new marriage alternative now that she was approaching sixty. She had just received a proposal from a very nice, caring and wonderful man who possessed all of the lifestyle qualities she had ever wanted: vacation homes, resources for unlimited travel and intellectual, stimulating friends. She said, "When I was in my early twenties, I only would consider marrying for love, but now I have to look at my future in a different way and consider my financial well-being. I also recognize I could very well spend the rest of my life alone." Although Jillian has no real "sizzle" for this man, she is opting for what she feels will be a very comfortable, companionable lifestyle.

Sometimes You Need to Make Hard Decisions

A large area of concern in the End Game of midlife dating can be health issues. Mickey, a woman in our study, fell head over heels in love with Carl. The problem? Only one—Carl had a history of serious heart disease and was not prone to take care of himself. Mickey had lost her first husband, after being married less than a year, in a car accident. And years later, her second husband died of cancer. She did not feel she could go through the anguish of losing another husband. Thus, she sorrowfully ended her relationship with Carl when it became clear to her he was not willing to take the necessary steps, such as proper diet and exercise, to help prevent another heart attack.

A Different Kind of Compromise

Joachim and Shannon are an example of how a couple successfully worked the End Game of a major relationship issue. Joachim had worked hard all his life and dreamed of retiring and moving to San Diego near a golf course. Shannon could not imagine life without her friends and family in Northern California. After some counseling and truly understanding how much their relationship meant to them, they were able to compromise. They agreed to spend six months during the winter in San Diego and six months during the summer in Northern California. Fortunately, their combined incomes allowed them to have two homes. They both sold their existing homes and agreed Joachim could select the San Diego house and Shannon would select the other.

Be Open to New Options

The issues are more clear cut when you arrive at the End Game. After all, today is tomorrow! The life-altering decisions of our early adulthood—how many children to have, career paths, life style—are issues of the past. Now we are faced with simpler, but important, relationship decisions. Where can we live the happiest? Do we agree on friends, activities and leisure time? How do we reconcile our faith and philosophy of life with a new partner? Once these issues are resolved, our maturity should allow our relationships to smoothly sail forward and gain that extra dimension needed for long-term success and fulfillment.

Quiz – Chapter Seventeen

During the End Game, it is time to reevaluate your attitude and consider new options. If you can do this, your relationship will have a greater chance for success. This quick quiz will help you evaluate where you are in the process. Please rate yourself as follows:

10 points for a "yes"; 5 points for an "undecided"; 0 points for a "no"

Ranking   Question

_____   1. I know what my number one goal is for the future.

_____   2. I realize many people who say, "I will never get married again" will ultimately change if the right person comes along.

_____   3. A high priority in my life is taking care of my health—this is reflected in my good diet and exercise program.

_____   4. In the End Game, I would gladly give full disclosure about my past life.

_____   5. I am aware that others' ingrained bad traits are hard to fix.

_____   6. I would leave a relationship if it was evident my partner's offensive behavior would not change.

_____   7. I would make compromises to make a good relationship work

Scoring

70 - 60 - You have things figured out and can adapt to the new game.

50 – 30 - You are very close to a clear understanding of the End Game.

20 – 0   - At least you know what's involved.

CHAPTER 18

Practical Decisions: Marriage, Live Apart or Live Together

""I am totally in love with Larry, but I don't want him underfoot all the time."
Beth

Once you and your partner have decided to make your relationship permanent, there are many practical decisions to be made. Getting married may be the simplest and most obvious thing to do and probably is the most likely result of successful End Game play. Most people believe that if they are fortunate enough to find love at second sight, they will do many things to keep the relationship viable, including making it permanent. However, as our survey shows, the attitudes of both men and women have changed and "commitment" today might well mean something other than marriage.

Many people in our study told us when they found unconditional love, they felt all other obstacles, no matter how large, could be overcome. Sam told us, "I met Sheila on a Sierra Club hike and knew at once she was the person for whom I had been searching forever. Our path towards marriage was long and sometimes rocky, but nevertheless, it was always a straight one. We both knew marriage was the answer." Others were not so convinced. A significant percentage of both men and women in our survey said their decision to marry "could go either way" or that marriage was "not important." But they did agree that staying together was their essential goal.

According to our study, once a couple decides they do want to spend the rest of their life together, it is the woman who pushes for marriage, but only by a very marginal percentage. The majority of both men and women tell us they would be just as happy and feel just as committed if they lived together without an actual marriage license. It is clear a committed relationship often has new meaning for those in midlife or older .

Our survey respondents gave us the following answers when asked, "Is it important for you to have a great relationship regardless of whether or not it leads to marriage?"

Category	Men's Response	Women's Response
Very important	48%	51%
Important	39%	34%
Could go either way	13%	12%
Not important	0%	3%

When we asked, "Is it important for you to get married again?" our respondents replied:

Category	Men's Response	Women's Response
Very important	8%	14%
Important	19%	19%
Could go either way	54%	45%
Not important	19%	22%

Interestingly, 87 percent of the men felt it was "very important" or "important" to have a great relationship, but when asked about marriage the numbers went to only 27 percent saying it was "very important" or "important."

Women gave similar answers, with 85 percent saying it was "very important" or "important" to have a great relationship and only 33 percent saying it was "very important" or "important" to be married.

The Survey Results May Surprise You

An astounding 73 percent of men and 67 percent of women said marriage "could go either way" or was "not important." Do you think a similar survey done with twenty- or thirty-year-olds would give this kind of result? This is a dramatic shift in ideology.

Darryl, a study member, told us he had reviewed the marriage vows: "Love until death, honor, cherish, do not commit adultery, perform husband or wifely duties, be faithful and loving" and felt he could practice these edicts in his relationship without marrying.

For some couples, getting married may actually complicate their relationships. This is why commitment, to some, does not include marriage. They are committed, but it does not include an actual marriage certificate. And that may not be a bad thing. Consider the following pluses and minuses.

Money Management Matters

Finances can play a huge role in deciding whether or not to get married. You may make the decision that it is wise not to co-mingle your assets due to family obligations or requirements. One of you may be receiving alimony and it will be lost if you remarry. Similarly, pension payments may be forfeited, particularly if you are a widow or widower receiving benefits from your former spouse's employer.

Although this book is not intended in any way to be a financial guide, there are other important considerations if you choose not to marry. For example, if you do not have a will that specifies your property is to go to your committed but unmarried partner, he or she will get nothing and your assets will automatically go to your relatives as dictated by state law.

One of the solutions to many of the financial problems you may encounter is revocable living trusts and wills, which can provide security for a current partner (married or not) in case of death or disability. In fact, if you decide not to get married and you have any assets you want to have distributed to your partner, creating a revocable living trust (which can easily be modified) is one of the easiest ways to insure he or she will be the recipient of any or all of your assets.

You can even make your partner the trustee of your living trust in the event of your death or permanent disability. Trustees or co-trustees can assure there is a proper succession of assets. If you are one of the many couples that choose not to be married, you can still insure the financial future of your partner with a variety of legal processes.

Avoid This Mistake

Dorothy lived for twelve years with Dennis, only to have him die unexpectedly. She was not named in his trust or will, although he always had told her he wanted her to have half of his assets. His children, who did not like Dorothy, claimed his entire estate. Sadly, Dorothy was forced out of the house and had to move out of state to live with her daughter. Dorothy had relied on Dennis's verbal good intentions. If you live with someone whom you are financially dependent upon, be sure you are protected. Do not become a Dorothy!

Health Issues Become Relevant

We received many health related stories of couples that could not make a go of it because one partner felt the other was not taking care of him or herself. Justin, after a year with Priscilla, decided he could not watch her abuse her body after she was told she had diabetes. She continued to eat the wrong foods and acted as though everything was normal, when in fact, she was dramatically shortening her life. A number of people said they would have stayed in their relationships if their partners had made a commitment to "do what the doctor ordered." Instead, they felt powerless when their partner simply refused to follow simple guidelines that would improve their health and longevity.

Assisting one another with health-related decisions is another important issue that unmarried couples need to address. Without a written health care proxy document that gives each partner the right to make medical decisions if the other is incapacitated, a person is powerless to help a partner and may not even be permitted to visit him or her in the hospital, as they are not considered a member of the legally-defined immediate family.

Lots of Little Details

There are several other practical issues to consider, such as homeowner's or renter's insurance, that should not be overlooked. If you are living with someone in your home and you haven't added him or her to your policy, any belongings of that individual destroyed by fire or other disasters will not be covered. Obviously, this will be true for you if you have moved into your partner's home. If you have an IRA or other retirement account and you want your partner to be the beneficiary, or vice versa, changes need to be made to the plan. These are just a few of the things that need your attention if you and your partner intend to spend the rest of your life together. Don't assume that just because you live together everything is okay legally and financially. It's not. Take the advice of attorneys and accountants so that both you and your partner are protected.

Some Are Happy Being Apart

Another consideration of whether to marry or not or live together or not is how you spend your time. Many couples at this stage of their lives have spent so much time establishing their own identities and daily routines that they just don't want the other person around all the time. To many this may seem an entirely foreign manner of thinking, but some people really need their own space. They just need and want to be on their own for part of the time. If you are the partner of one of these people and you are not happy with this arrangement, you may have a serious problem.

Beth is a fifty-three-year-old former insurance executive who is in love with Larry, but doesn't want him around all the time. She is totally in love with him, they do lots of things together and spend part of most days together, but she is not sure if she wants him with her every single day. Larry does not relate to this kind of logic and has a difficult time understanding why, on any given evening, she will suggest that he go home or tells him she wants to be alone for a day or two to pursue her own activities.

This is fairly common behavior when one of the partners has been single for a long period of time. He or she is accustomed to a certain amount of independence and even though there is a strong commitment to the happiness of the other partner, such individuals need time to be physically apart.

Don't Let Your Ego Get In the Way of the Relationship

If you find yourself in a situation in which you want to either marry or live together, but your partner doesn't, you may have to be content with the decision to live apart in deference to him or her. Bide your time and persevere and, possibly, you eventually can persuade your partner to wed or cohabit. One of the things you should not do is let your ego get in the way and issue an ultimatum to your partner. Many in our survey commented that this seldom works.

If you recall, this was the case with Sarah, whose move to Los Angeles led to her current state of abject unhappiness. So before you act in haste, consider the fact that living apart may not be so bad after all——at least you have a loving partner who makes you happy and that is certainly better than the alternative. The biggest thing you need to overcome is an ego that makes you decide to abandon the relationship for the wrong reason. Time and time again, people who sever what is an otherwise wonderful relationship go out into the world looking for someone new and find it is not so easy. Think about what commitment means to you before you act.

The Advantages Outweigh the Disadvantages

Consider what a great opportunity exists when you are starting again in your later years. First, you have a great chance to establish a relationship in which compromise replaces the contention that may have existed in your prior relationships. This means no arguments over things that were (or at least seemed) important in your younger years. You no longer will argue over money, (it is a statistical fact that the number one argument couples have during their married lives has involved money), children or what to do with your free time—these issues are gone (if they are not, you may want to consider why you are in this relationship). It is inconceivable that any couple in our dating category, contemplating a long-term relationship would not have had this discussion.

The reason you are together and have reached the point of being in the End Game stage of the midlife dating game presumably is because you understand the mistakes you made in prior relationships and have learned to avoid them in this relationship.

People who get together in their later years have the potential to avoid most of the conflicts of their first, second or, if you have been that active, third relationships (more than that and you really are not paying attention). It is a matter of understanding both yourself and the details of the other person's life. Use his or her *history* to guide you in making intelligent decisions.

Shawn, a survey participant, fell in love with Virginia at first sight. He soon discovered she had one very annoying habit: She liked to sleep late and, when she got up, had a hard time getting going. He, on the other hand, was a morning person and found it exceedingly difficult to just hang around while he waited for Virginia to become conversant. He told us, "I would not have put up with this in an earlier relationship, but I am now sixty-five and I would rather have a companion, even if she's not available in the early morning." Fortunately, they both were able to make adjustments and the relationship flourished. It's really amazing what maturity does for a relationship.

It takes two people who don't exist in a world of ego and who have learned to communicate with one another in an open manner to create a successful partnership. Certainly it is normal for a relationship to suffer some dissension, but it should not, at this stage in life, be cause for a breakup. Honest discussion and a bit of compromise should do the trick. If some issue is so great you just can't tolerate being together all of the time, implement one of the other options discussed in this chapter. Who says you have to be together every day and night?

Are Your Values the Same?

Most people we interviewed agreed that when selecting a permanent partner, it is important to have similar values. When we asked our study members what they valued most in their life today, they listed things that at this stage of their life they felt should be ongoing.

Men valued:	
good health	(43%)
friends	(21%)
family	(15%)
financial security	(11%)
time to enjoy life	(10%)

One man told us, "I almost died of a heart attack last year. Now I enjoy each day as a gift and take better care of myself more than ever." With "good health" being the overwhelming high scorer with 43 percent saying it is of primary importance, men are learning they are not invincible. Maybe that is a reason they are also more prone to consider committed relationships than they were in their youth. Yes, the clock is ticking, the boat is leaving the dock and men want to be on board.

Women valued:	
family	(31%)
friends	(27%)
good health	(24%)
financial security	(10%)
freedom to do as I please	(8%)

The results were very interesting, with both men and women essentially agreeing on what was most important in their lives today. The last items, "time to enjoy life" for men and "freedom to do as I please" for women, could be interpreted to mean the same thing. Many women clearly relish their independence from domestic or parental responsibilities, meaning they are now enjoying life. Is it possible that in midlife men and women finally are getting in sync with one another?

A Significant Event Can Change Your Mind

David had been single for nearly twenty years after the death of his wife. He was content with his seven-year relationship with Angela and had no wish to marry again, even though she did. What made him change his mind? During a hike in Yosemite, he slipped on a wet rock and fell ten feet down into a ravine. He broke his back and Angela never left his side while he was in the hospital. After he was released, she moved in with him for a month to care for him, bringing him his meals in bed and meeting his every need.

During this time, David realized he couldn't imagine not being married to her for the rest of his life. As soon as he got the cast off his back and was able to get out of bed, he dropped to his knees and begged her to marry him. For him the decision of living together, marrying or continuing to live apart became irrelevant. Angela had come through for him and he knew he wanted to be with her as much as possible and to do his best to make her happy. Marriage was the best answer for the both of them.

You Are Not Alone

There are millions of men and women in the world in exactly the same situation as you, many of them probably voicing the same regrets: "I should have…" or "If only I had…" Don't be full of regret. The next time you see someone interesting, start by just saying hello. It can be as simple as that!

Once you find that great relationship, the End Game takes place whether you live apart, live together or get married. Most of our respondents said that if they were lucky enough to have found that perfect person, they would do whatever it took to stay in the relationship. While marriage seems like the perfect ending, there are other excellent options. What matters is being together and being there for each other. If you set realistic goals and the chemistry exists, you can have that once-, twice- or thrice-in-a-lifetime opportunity to catch the magic ring and begin anew.

Quiz – Chapter Eighteen

How exciting! You are now coming to some of the most important decisions you will ever make. Do you know if you want to be married, live together or live apart? This quick quiz will help you evaluate where you are in this process. Please rate yourself as follows:

10 points for a "yes"; 5 points for an "undecided"; 0 points for a "no"

Ranking	Question
_____	1. I understand commitment means different things to different people and I know my definition.
_____	2. I have made a past commitment to another person and can do so again.
_____	3. It is important for me to have a great relationship in my life.
	4. Getting married again is a high priority for me, but I would be willing to forgo this for a committed relationship.
_____	5. I am able to give my partner space in a relationship and not feel threatened.
_____	6. My relationship priorities are different now than when I was twenty and I am able to articulate them clearly.
_____	7. I understand the legal and financial ramifications of living together and have taken or will take steps to protect my partner and myself.

Scoring

70 – 60 - You seem ready to move forward in a relationship.

50 – 30 - You are undecided. But you are becoming aware that it is time to make a move.

20 – 0 - Something is holding you back, you may need more time to reflect on the issues.

CHAPTER 19

Finding Your Soul Mate

"From the first time I saw her, I experienced a profound sense of connection."
Dwight

W hat is different about a "soul mate" relationship than any other love relationship? Not everyone in our study, even those who say they have been
in love numerous times and have been married, tell us they feel they have truly
experienced this kind of relationship. And when they hear of others having
met a soul mate, they wonder, *Is this a dream that is obtainable for me?*

Soul Mates Are Unique

While there are many definitions of a soul mate, the best description seems to
be that soul mates are life partners with whom we feel an indescribable bond
of closeness and comfort. They are, in essence, an extension of our own minds
and thought processes. Finding a soul mate has been described as a mystical
experience, with two people becoming instantly attracted, mentally and physically, and accompanied by the feeling they are destined to be together. Love
in this case is a given and it is seemingly everlasting. Shakespeare said: "No
sooner met, but they looked. No sooner looked, but they loved." One cannot
find a more apt description of soul mates discovering one another.

Soul Mates Aren't Always Found

Some people in our study who have never had a soul mate were dubious that this concept was even viable. They took a more pragmatic view, believing romance needs time to bloom and a period of getting to know the other person is absolutely necessary. While stories of soul mates finding each other are uplifting and filled with the excitement of the profound possibilities, not everyone will find one. A good number of our survey respondents told us they spent many years married to or living with mates they deeply loved and were content with in every way, but did not believe they were matched with their soul mates. However, they stated they were very happy and would not trade their partners for anyone.

It's an Exciting Experience

We asked those in our study who had experienced a soul mate relationship to describe their feelings. Dwight, one of our oldest participants, told us, "In my opinion, a soul mate relationship is one that stands the test of time. I am in my eighties and although my wife, Marian, died a few years ago, we continued to grow even closer each day until her death. For me, from the moment I first saw her, I experienced a profound sense of connection."

Alice gave us her definition: "It is instant familiarity. When I met Michael, I experienced a strong shock of recognition. It was as if we had met before and I felt I already knew everything about him. While we never married, we were together constantly for thirty years until he died five years ago."

Finding a soul mate is one of the most exciting, meaningful experiences you will ever have. However, such a relationship demands a high level of intensity and interaction. People look at those who have found a soul mate with wonder. They are envious. They want to know, "Where and how did they find each other?" They also question, "Are soul mates happier people? Are they healthier because they take better care of each other? Are they so attuned to one another that their life is always wonderful even in times of hardship or sorrow?"

Fate May Play a Role

Some people believe fate brings soul mates together. Joanna said, "I would never have met Peter, my true soul mate, if I had not missed my plane to Denver. There was a terrible storm and the roads were icy and dangerous. Traffic was piled up and by the time I got to the airport and checked in, the plane was just departing. But then there was Peter, hair and scarf flying, and he was rushing to catch the flight also. We were both upset the flight had departed without us and we decided to have coffee together while we waited four hours for the next plane.

"As they say, the rest is history. Meeting Peter was the deepest and most profound experience I have ever had. We both felt such an intensity of connection that we knew then and there we would spend the rest of our lives together."

Extensions of Each Other

Sue, who is in her late fifties, told us, "In my first real relationship, large events such as birthdays, holidays and other meaningful celebrations seemed to give structure to our lives. Then I got divorced and was single for a number of years. When I met my soul mate, the small, unimportant events were what gave meaning and caused our souls to prosper. We now believe the soul needs quiet time to ponder and grow."

Leslie told us what many others had. Once she met her soul mate, they cut through a lot of the normal, preliminary posturing and tentative communicating in their dating, because they knew from the start they were right for each other. They each had a high level of trust and almost felt as if the other person was an extension of their own bodies.

Past Intensity Makes Re-starting More Painful

Nancy, who had a soul mate who died, recalls the evening when they first met. She was at a party and simply gravitated to a tall, handsome man named Bill. After about thirty minutes, he leaned over and said, "You know I am going to marry you, don't you?" The feeling was so powerful that all Nancy could do was nod.

Many study participants discussed the death of a soul mate and echoed similar feelings. One woman said, "Even thirty years after my soul mate died, I remember everything about the relationship as vividly as when we still were together. And the longing to be with my soul mate again is just as strong."

A Passionate Relationship

A soul mate relationship is passionate mentally, physically and emotionally. It can make you feel more loved than ever before. And it can also make you feel more understood. Soul mates see the value in the other person; they see each other's worth. Said one woman, "Doug and I had a terrific mutual admiration society. This feeling gave us an incredible support system."

Nat told us of his experience with his soul mate. "When I met Pam, I was never so happy. I had recently retired and had not experienced such a strong feeling for another person before. We were deeply content and longed to hold on to the moment forever. But we soon realized change is inevitable. We could not freeze the moment; we all evolve.

"When I started to grow in a new direction, Pam resisted my growth and our relationship almost reached a crisis. Then we realized true soul mates encourage each other and we agreed not to be threatened by new interests or directions. This kind of love was a new experience and adventure for both of us. It was at this time in my life I experienced the most self-discovery as well as the greatest joy."

Finding a Soul Mate Is a Life-changing Experience

Kathleen told us, "When I met my soul mate, it was a mysterious phenomenon, a complex richness that touched every bit of my being. I was never lonely again, nor did I ever feel so secure." Almost without exception, those in our study who told us they had a soul mate said the relationship broke up only because of death. Many said they had been in numerous other relationships since, and even in loving marriages, but had never again experienced the deep connection of their original soul mate. It seems to be a connection that only happens once in a lifetime. Those who fell in love with someone who had a previous soul mate told us they never truly felt they were able to measure up to that person.

Randall said, "When I met my soul mate, we decided to get married in a very short time. One night over dinner, I took out two pieces of paper and asked her to make a list of all the positive events she felt would occur if she married me. Then I asked her to make a list of all the negative events. I did the same. When we compared our lists, thirty minutes later, the deal was clinched. We had both listed about twenty great reasons why we should be together forever and neither of us had listed a negative. It was a no-brainer and that very night we set our wedding date."

Amanda said, "Souls want to be connected and when they meet similar souls, they form profound bonds. I instantly communicated with my newly found soul mate, not with words, but by intimate gestures, a flick of the hand, a nod of the head. We understood each other completely. In my opinion, souls want to be attached and embraced."

An Overwhelming Need to Bond

Kenneth shared his experience with us. "I was forty-seven when I met my soul mate. When I saw Sharon, the need for intimacy with this beautiful woman was just overwhelming. I suddenly realized she was the first woman in my life to whom I wanted to reveal my innermost self and she was the first person I trusted enough to do this. What I found equally amazing was that in this sharing, I came to know not only Sharon better, but also my own self."

Most of our participants who had experienced soul mate relationships indicated they were unusually smooth ones. Said Art, "Marty and I would go to functions and sometimes see other couples fighting or arguing. We understood each other so well that we rarely had a cross word between us. Sure, we had differences of opinion, but we were always able to discuss our feelings while being highly tuned in to each other. I held Marty in such high regard that the idea of yelling or losing my temper with her never crossed my mind."

Rachel told us about her experience. "I had always been scared to death of commitment. But once I met Ben, I just trusted him on an almost gut-level. I was sure he was the right person for me and I entered the relationship with the knowledge that we could make it work. He was very gentle and sensitive to my needs. I trusted him completely—a real first for me. Ben just had a certain look, a familiar smile and a twinkle in his eye that drew me to him like a magnet. As far as I was concerned, my world revolved around him.

"We had fifteen glorious years together before he died in a freak boating accident. Our relationship had grown stronger each year. We could finish each other's sentences and I always knew what he was thinking by just looking into his eyes. I have begun dating again, as I know Ben would want me to get out and be happy. But I have yet to find anyone I feel even remotely as connected to as I did to Ben. If you are lucky enough to have found a soul mate, it is a one-time occurrence in your lifetime."

It Touches All Phases of Your Life

The people in our study who have experienced a soul mate relationship summarize it by saying, "Having a soul mate is a mysterious phenomenon, a complex richness that touches all phases of our being. The intimacy of the relationship keeps us from being lonely and it makes us feel secure. Having a soul mate helps us understand who we are and it helps us integrate the past, present and future into a meaningful and unifying life. In short, it gives us our identity." Added one, "Once you have lost a soul mate, you miss him or her every day of your life." Another said, "If you are one of the fortunate ones in life who finds a soul mate, there is no question of whether or not you should spend the rest of your life together—it is just a given."

Those who have found soul mates say it is the most powerful and joyous relationship experience of their lives. A soul mate brings your heart alive. We hope each of our readers will be so lucky.

On the other hand, many people in our study who have not had a soul mate experience believe that finding one is not a requirement for happiness. They advise not to obsess about searching for a soul mate to the detriment of other relationship opportunities that also can make you feel happy and fulfilled.

Quiz – Chapter Nineteen

If you find a soul mate, are you prepared to make that deep and joyous connection? To be with someone who is almost an extension of your own body? This quiz will give you some insight into your own readiness. Please rate yourself as follows:

10 points for a "yes"; 5 points for an "undecided"; 0 points for a "no"

Ranking   Question

_____   1. I hope to find a soul mate sometime in my life.

_____   2. I now have, or have had in the past, a true soul mate.

_____   3. I have observed other people in this kind of relationship so I know it exists.

_____   4. I believe soul mates are accidental occurrences and you can't look for one, but you can hope to find one.

_____   5. I know I would feel an immediate sense of connection with a soul mate.

_____   6. A soul mate relationship would be too intense at this point in my life and I am not particularly interested in finding one.

_____   7. I am not trying to find a soul mate; I don't think they exist and I just want a normal relationship.

Scoring
70 – 60 - You have the right mindset and have the possibility of soul mates in perspective.

50 – 30 - You have your eyes open for a soul mate, but you are realistic.

20 – 0 - You feel that a relationship is a relationship and you are content with that.

CHAPTER 20

In Conclusion

The two key messages of this book are: "Don't give up" and "Get out there." Pari, a woman Mason knows who is famous for her matchmaking skills, tried for two years to find the perfect match for a fifty-two-year-old male friend. He told her, "I want a woman I can be happy with for the rest of my life"

After seventy-five blind dates, it happened—his perfect woman appeared in his life. *Seventy-five blind dates?* Is this obsessive? Maybe so, but no one said finding a perfect relationship is easy. As Pari is fond of saying, "There is a lid for every pot. It just takes some time and effort."

Do What Works for You

As we have said throughout this book, "If you want to find someone, you need to be noticed." Granted, some of you will say, "That is just too much work," and will retreat to what is comfortable and decline to participate in what appears to be a Herculean effort. That is certainly an option. Some men and women do live perfectly happy lives without partners.

But before you reject all the options that are open to you to find a relationship, remember the middle ground that we discussed in chapter 2. Omit having many blind dates if you are not comfortable with that option, but follow the example of Adrian, Carol, Bruce, Ralph, Camille, Ruth, Marge and Hanna and take advantage of social situations as they occur to meet new people. Theirs were meetings of opportunity that only happened because one of the parties was willing to initiate a conversation and the other person was open enough to respond.

As you must have learned from this book by now, a positive, open attitude coupled with self-confidence will certainly go a long way in helping you realize your objective. Being proactive and just letting people know you exist is all it may take—it's amazing what can happen. Remember, many others are just as shy as you are about approaching the opposite sex. There is a high probability they are very open to just having you say "Hello, that's a great tie" or "Nice outfit" as an opening to a conversation. So, to borrow a phrase from the sports world—just do it.

The Primary "Want" and "Don't Want" Qualities Have Changed

Keep in mind the differences in what men and woman are looking for at this age. While much of what men and women want in the opposite sex has remained the same, the priorities have changed. It is also important to remember that what one person sees in another will vary greatly, so there is not a standard definition for any of these traits.

The men in our study overwhelmingly stated they now want someone who is compatible with them and has common interests. They also look for a woman who is attractive and intelligent. The other qualities they look for are sexuality and the abilities to have fun and support themselves. While men still place attractiveness near the top of their list, they put sexuality down near the bottom of desired qualities— something that ironically may now be discouraging to the many women who moved "sexual" and "romantic" up to number one on their list of desired traits. This new view by women about sex may be a surprise to many men who thought they had a monopoly on this quality.

The women in our study indicated they now want men who are romantic and sexual, with intelligence and who are financially secure. They then look for a sense of humor, spiritual awareness and those who are loyal and thoughtful. The fact that "sexual" wasn't even in the top six when they were younger marks one of the dramatic ways in which women's attitudes have changed as they have become more secure and self-aware. The good news is both genders reported that sex is still as good as in their earlier years.

We'll Say It Again. Learn to Communicate.

In the final analysis it appears that regardless of the changes in the views of men and women from youth to midlife, both essentially want a secure, trusting relationship in which both parties are able to communicate with one another about what is important. It's that simple.

This is not brain surgery. Our rules for playing the midlife dating game simply say to use your maturity to understand yourself, analyze your potential partner, and make an informed decision. Emotion is not to be discarded, but used as only one element in the total equation. Stories of men and women meeting in midlife and having a wonderful life together abound. There is no reason one of the stories cannot be your own. Just don't give up—tomorrow is here!

APPENDIX

Questionnaire Results

We decided to do this questionnaire as a supplement to our interviews with over 1,000 single people in their middle years and older regarding their experiences with midlife dating and relationships. We felt qualified to do this as both of us fit the guidelines of our readership and our survey respondents.

The questionnaire was first sent to singles groups in the San Francisco Bay Area. To expand our base, we then sent it to other selected singles across the United States. Respondents also included our individual single friends and many of their friends. The only criteria for filling out the questionnaire was that the respondent be single and in midlife. No scientific analysis was made of the respondent population and we did not ask our participants to identify themselves. Over half of our survey questionnaires were returned, over 400 in all, constituting one of the largest samples studying the midlife dating phenomenon. Many respondents signed their names and said they were willing let us use their stories, however, all names have been changed except for those who granted permission for their real names to be used. Out of this research, certain valid and interesting conclusions have been drawn.

"Love At Second Sight – Playing The midlife Dating Game"

Questionnaire Results

1. Are you male or female?
    Male   180 (45%)
    Female   220 (55%)

2. How many times have you been married?
    a. Men

1.	Never	13%
2.	Once	64%
3.	Twice	22%
4.	Three or more	1%

    b. Women

1.	Never	12%
2.	Once	59%
3.	Twice	26%
4.	Three or more	3%

3. Most frequently mentioned qualities looked for in first marriage:
    a. Men

1.	Attractive, popular, social, fit	40%
2.	Romantic, sexual	21%
3.	Similar background	16%
4.	Family oriented	13%
5.	Educated & intelligent	10%

    b. Women

1.	Good provider	30%
2.	Intelligent	25%
3.	Companionship	17%
4.	Romantic, sexual	15%
5.	Qualities for good father	13%

4. Now that I am older and single, qualities I look for are:

    a. Men

1. Common interests	34%
2. Attractive	22%
3. Intelligent, educated	17%
4. Romantic, sexual	13%
5. Fun, into a lot of activities	9%
6. Can support self	5%

    b. Women

1. Romantic, sexual	36%
2. Educated, intelligent	28%
3. Financially secure	19%
4. Sense of humor	8%
5. Spiritual knowledge	6%
6. Loyal and thoughtful (tied)	3%

5. Are you in a relationship now?

    a. Men

1. Yes	56%
2. No	44%

    b. Women

1. Yes	33%
2. No	67%

6. Most frequently mentioned words which describe the current relationship:

    a. Men

1. Sizzling and sexy	35%
2. Compatible, comfortable	26%
3. Sense of humor	11%
4. Supportive of me	15%
5. Trusting	8%
6. Stimulating	5%

  b. Women

1.	Committed to me	33%
2.	Equal partner	25%
3.	Common values	14%
4.	Shared activities	14%
5.	Integrity	8%
6.	Spiritual	6%

7. How important is it to get married again?

  a. Men

1.	Very important	8%
2.	Important	18%
3.	I could go either way	54%
4.	Not important	20%

  b. Women

1.	Very important	14%
2.	Important	19%
3.	I could go either way	45%
4.	Not important	22%

8. How important is it to have a great relationship (which may not lead to marriage?)

  a. Men

1.	Very important	48%
2.	Important	39%
3.	I could go either way	13%
4.	Not important	0

  b. Women

1.	Very important	51%
2.	Important	34%
3.	I could go either way	12%
4.	Not important	3%

9. Why did your most recent relationship or marriage end?

a. Men

1. Chemistry ended — 32%
2. Poor communication — 24%
3. Problems within the family — 17%
4. Goals became divergent — 14%
5. She always had to be right — 10%
6. Wanted to raise her grandchildren and I did not — 3%

b. Women

1. Drifted apart — 26%
2. He had affair, flame went out — 24%
3. Too controlling — 21%
4. Put his interests before mine — 15%
5. Financial priorities differed — 12%
6. He was immature and wouldn't grow up — 2%

10. What would you do differently in your next relationship or marriage?

a. Men

1. I don't know — 31%
2. Take more time before making commitment — 26%
3. Make a better choice — 18%
4. Communicate my feelings clearer — 12%
5. Not dwell on the negatives — 8%
6. Give her more support — 5%

b. Women

1. I don't know — 35%
2. Be clearer on what I want — 24%
3. Not fall in love so quickly — 17%
4. Leave sooner when I knew it was over — 12%
5. Maintain more independence — 9%
6. Not expect so much — 3%

11. Do you normally select your relationship partners or do they select you?

    a.   Men
        1. I select   32%
        2. They select   16%
        3. Mutual   52%

    b.   Women
        1. I select   5%
        2. They select   24%
        3. Mutual   71%

12. How many years did your longest committed relationship or marriage last?

    a.   Men – 18, 16, 12 (in order of years most commonly listed) Average – 18.1

    b.   Women – 7, 15, 20 (in order of years most commonly listed) Average - 16.6

13. How many years did your shortest committed relationship or marriage last?

    a.   Men – 1, 4, 2 (in order of years most commonly listed) Average – 3.4

    b.   Women – 1, 2, 3 (in order of years most commonly listed) Average – Women 2.5

14. How many truly committed relationships have you had other than marriage?

    a.   Men
        1. One   26%
        2. Two   21%
        3. Three to five   34%
        4. Five to ten   11%
        5. Over ten   8%

    b.   Women
        1. One   12%
        2. Two   33%

3. Three to five	45%
4. Five to ten	8%
5. Over ten	2%

15. In your best relationship, what was the difference in age, who was older?
   a. Men – Man older by 8.6 years on average
      1. 86% of men said they were older;
      2. 14% said they were younger

   b. Women – Man older by 5.1 years on average
      1. 19% of women said they were older;
      2. 81% said they were younger

16. How many years younger are you willing to date someone?
   a. Men –   15.4 years

   b. Woman –   7.1 years

17. How many years older are you willing to date someone?
   a. Men –   2.4 years

   b. Women –   8.3 years

18. Best places to find congenial people in midlife?
   a. Men

1. Still searching!	33%
2. Special interest groups (hiking, skiing, book clubs, bridge, etc.)	26%
3. Singles organizations	19%
4. Church events	11%
5. Internet	11%

   b. Women

1. Wish I knew!	31%
2. Mutual friends	25%
3. Special interest groups (hiking, skiing, book clubs, bridge, etc.)	19%
4. Singles organizations	16%

5. College reunions	9%

19. What do you value most in your life now?

   a. Men

1. Good health	43%
2. Friends	21%
3. Family	15%
4. Financial security	11%
5. Time to enjoy life	10%

   b. Women

1. Family	31%
2. Friends	27%
3. Good health	24%
4. Financial stability	10%
5. Freedom to do as I please	8%

20. What is your number one goal for the future?

   a. Men

1. Find a partner	34%
2. Stay healthy	24%
3. Live an active life	16%
4. Keep learning	11%
5. Become more footloose	7%
6. Help others	4%
7. Be happy	4%

   b. Women

1. Find a safe, secure relationship	32%
2. Be healthy	17%
3. Financial security	15%
4. Live a long life	12%
5. Personal growth	10%
6. Make a difference	8%
7. Follow a spiritual path	6%